WHIZZBANGS AND WOODBINES

TALES OF WORK AND PLAY ON THE WESTERN FRONT

A VILLAGE CALVARY AT THE FRONT.

WHIZZBANGS AND WOODBINES

TALES OF WORK AND PLAY ON THE WESTERN FRONT

BY THE

REV. J. C. V. DURELL, B.D.

RECTOR OF ROTHERHITHE, AND CHIEF COM-
MISSIONER OF THE CHURCH ARMY IN FRANCE

UNIFORM

UNIFORM

First published by Hodder and Stoughton in 1918
This edition first published by Uniform in 2018
an imprint of Unicorn Publishing Group

Unicorn Publishing Group
101 Wardour Street
London W1F 0UG
www.unicornpublishing.org

A catalogue record for this book is available from the British Library

ISBN 978-1-910500-22-4

Printed and bound in Great Britain

Please note: *In producing in facsimile from original historical documents, any
imperfections may be reproduced and the quality may be lower than modern
typesetting or cartographic standards.*

PREFACE

THESE cameo pictures of a soldier's life in work
and recreation on the Western Front have been
drawn by one who, as Church Army Commissioner in France, has had special opportunities
for travel up and down behind the lines. My
work has brought me into contact both with
the men in the recreation huts and also with
the military authorities at Army Head-quarters
and Divisional Head-quarters in the various
sections of the area in which my work lay. My
relations with the chaplains also have been close
and intimate and always most happy and cordial.
I have thus had opportunities of hearing and
seeing things from the point of view both of the
officers and men, and I have tried to catch and
to reflect something of the spirit that inspires
our armies in France.

Some of these pages have already appeared in
substance in *The Church Times* and in *The
Treasury Magazine*. I wish to thank the proprietors for their courtesy in allowing me to
reproduce them here.

J. C. V. DURELL.

CONTENTS

CHAPTER I

CONTENTS

ILLUSTRATIONS

CHAPTER I

THE STREAM OF WAR

To those who knew France before the war it is,
indeed, a strange experience to go over the old
familiar ground and see how completely all is
changed. From the moment of leaving the
English port everything is different. Can this
really be the old Channel steamboat of other
days? Its decks are thronged with soldiers
of every kind, returning from leave or forming
new drafts for their regiments; there are large
numbers of Red Cross nurses coming out to join
their units; there are Church Army workers,
also in khaki, crossing to France to do the work
for the soldiers which it is my present purpose
to describe: all forming one conglomerate mass,
packed so closely together on the decks that

when once one has found a square foot to stand on it is impossible to move elsewhere. " *J'y suis, j'y reste !* " is the motto of the Channel crossing ! So there we stood, all of us wearing a strange new pattern of life-belt as a precaution against accidents.

No mishap however occurred, and indeed it is difficult to see how any such could be possible, so complete is the control which the British exercise over the Channel. Everywhere this is in evidence. Airships are overhead exploring the surface of the sea in this direction or that, ready always to drop their depth charges on any submarine that may be seen below. Destroyers, springing apparently from nowhere and rushing through the waves at tremendous speed, suddenly appear in readiness to guard the passing ships. Mine sweepers in pairs are engaged in clearing the waters of danger; and, through it all, the food ships all the time are passing on their way to some English port. It is a wonderful revelation how that, while the U-boats are doing their worst, Britain, none the less, is still Mistress of the Seas. It is strange to see the shipping, camouflaged for the most part in strange colours, blue and white and brown and black, in sweeps and waves and rays, designed to confuse vision and to make it difficult to estimate the speed at which the boat is travelling. And so it is that, protected by the strong arm of British sea power, we land in France.

How strange on landing to find the whole of this part of France under English control! Khaki everywhere; the streets policed by " red caps," as they are familiarly called; military police directing the traffic in the narrow alleys and round dangerous corners, flashing electric torches at night on the passers-by to see that no unauthorised person is out-of-doors after dark, directing lost parties which way they should go. There is a vast amount of examination of passports at every possible opportunity before one is allowed to reach one's destination; and, having once got there, there is no getting away again without all kinds of permission being obtained from Provost Marshals, Town Majors, Chief Commissioners, and all sorts of other officials invented for the purpose of carrying on a modern war. You can't just walk into a booking-office and ask for a ticket, and then get into a train! No, here I am, and here I must stay till the powers that be move me on.

From the moment of landing the new-comer must be filled with astonishment when he begins to realise what the maintenance and training of the British Army involves. Throughout the length of the quays at each Channel port enormous accumulations of military stores are stacked. Warehouse after warehouse is seen filled to its utmost capacity with all the multitudinous articles of supply which the maintenance of the Army requires. Packing cases of every size and variety are piled up in every direction. If we make a friend of the A.M.F.O. (Assistant Military Forwarding Officer) he will take us to a shed, in which we shall find stacked a number of cases labelled "Church Army." We shall see later on, as we look into the life of the huts, the purpose which the contents of these cases are destined to serve. We shall find that they contain such things as biscuits, tea, cigarettes, and tobacco ; in fact, all such things as help to supply the necessities, or add to the amenities, of a soldier's life. We shall notice that many of these cases are addressed to the Church Army Commissioner at one or other of the Front Headquarters, which act as distributing centres to the huts immediately behind the line.

But what a tremendous work all this immense and complicated transport must involve! We wonder how this vast accumulation of goods can ever be extricated from the apparent confusion and brought to its destination. Practically the whole of this work of distribution is in English hands. English rolling stock has been brought across the Channel to supply the need. Everywhere we see huge locomotive engines bearing the large letters R.O.D. (Railway Ordnance

Department). These English engines, which used to run on our main lines at home, are now engaged in carrying supplies to our troops along the railways of Northern France.

The heavy ambulance trains which fill many of the sidings are also British. These trains are waiting in the depôt, ready to go up to the Front, when required, to bring the wounded back to the Base. And wonderful trains they are, travelling so smoothly that one is hardly conscious of the motion. A corridor runs down the centre of the long coaches, and the beds for the wounded are ranged in tiers on either side, like bunks on board ship. Doctors, orderlies and nurses are carried on the train, and in one car is an operating theatre, so that emergency needs may at once be dealt with.

During a certain period of my work in France, it was part of my job to visit all the hospital trains that passed through a certain important railway-station. The trains stopped there for about ten minutes to enable the engine to take in water. This gave one an opportunity to go on board and see something of the men. My helpers came with me laden with boxes of cigarettes to give out to the wounded.

" See, lad," a worker would say, " here is a packet of Woodbines for you, a present from the Church Army. I will put it on your pillow and you can light up when you feel up to it, later on."

So we went from one to another down the long length of the train. And how the men appreciated the gifts! It was not their intrinsic value, for, as all the world at the Front knows, you can buy a packet of ten Woodbines for fifteen centimes, provided you belong to the B.E.F. It was rather the thought that the men were not forgotten and that friends in Blighty wanted, however inadequately, to show honour to the lads who had given so much to their country. And, after all, Woodbines on a hospital train are to be preferred to Whizzbangs in the trenches!

2

We always stayed on board the train till the last moment and jumped off when it began to move out of the station. If it happened to be at night, when all was pitch dark and no lights showing outside the cars, it was difficult to know when the train had started, so imperceptible was its gentle motion. We often had visions of being carried on to the next station!

However, by dint of employing an orderly to keep a look-out and to be ready to open the door for us when we rushed towards it, we managed to escape this fate.

Many of the wounded are taken down to the Base on Red Cross barges on the canals by the Inland Water Transport system. This is a very slow method, sometimes involving a week of travel, but it is beautifully comfortable. The canal system of Northern France is very complete and efficient, and full use is made of it for military purposes.

THE SOLDIER IN TRAINING

CHAPTER II

THE SOLDIER IN TRAINING

In Northern France huge British encampments are everywhere to be found. Big hotels are now all turned into hospitals. On our way up to the Front we shall find every variety of concentration of troops in rest or in training. There are rest camps, reinforcements camps, labour camps; there are Army schools for every conceivable purpose : gas schools, signal schools, trench mortar schools, Lewis gun schools, balloon schools, wiring schools, bombing schools, and so on, endlessly. There is even a school for chaplains. And to this latter the Chaplains to the Forces are sent from time to time for a week of rest and retreat.

I once met a very junior chaplain who was on

his way to spend a week at the school. He was most anxious that there should be no misconception as to its purpose. " You see," he explained to me, " it has to be called a school, because that is the military term, and it is only as such that it is able to obtain a military grant for maintenance. But of course it isn't really a school; we don't really go there to learn our job." This young man, who had been out in France about six months, was quite convinced that what he didn't know about his work was not worth knowing; and any suggestion of going to school to learn was completely foreign to his ideas.

This is, however, by the way. The frame of mind exhibited by this youth was in no way typical of the chaplains in France. They are almost all of them eager to learn, and it is this fact which is giving their work so high a value. The Church Army huts provide the chaplains with splendid opportunities for coming into close and intimate contact with the men. Again and again senior chaplains have said to me how greatly they find their work handicapped if they come into an area which is ill supplied with Church Army huts.

But primarily our huts are centres of recreation and places of rest.   And it will be recognised how great is the need for the work of voluntary associations, such as the Church Army, when it is remembered that practically the only alternative for the soldier is to be found in the French *estaminets*, where the atmosphere is not always of the best.   And, moreover, there has probably been no more fruitful field of operations for German spies.   A soldier's conversation is not always carefully guarded, and military information, of which the enemy has shown himself to be possessed, has probably been frequently gleaned in this way.   And so it has come about that the high military authorities have, from every point of view, been anxious to encourage in every possible way the provision of centres of recreation by the various voluntary organisa-

tions now at work in France.   They feel that
the life of these huts has given them very
real help in carrying out the spirit of the training which our men are receiving behind the
Front.

Let us remember that the purpose of British
military training is the development of individual
initiative.   In this, it differs from the German
ideal, which is one of blind obedience.   The
German aim is to produce the frame of mind
which leads men to go forward in massed formation, wave after wave, to almost certain destruction.   The British aim, on the other hand, is to
produce not a mere cog in a machine but a
thinking individual.   The men are taught
self-reliance; they are told that decisions
have to be taken not only by company commanders, or even N.C.O's, but often by the
men themselves, and with this end in view the
intelligence of the men is being constantly
trained in the various schools of which we
have spoken.

But if this training is to be effective, it is
evident that the moral of the men must be kept
high. And it is just at this point that the
military importance of our Church Army huts
comes in. It makes just all the difference to the
tone and spirit of the man, whether, after his
hours of work and training, he is obliged to go
to a low-class *estaminet*, or whether he can find
himself in the atmosphere created by a Church
Army hut. In these huts he is able to get
healthy recreation. He is able to listen to
lectures and take part in debates. He gets
away from the drill sergeant, and is able to
come into close and intimate contact with
the Hut Superintendent or with the chaplain
who makes use of that particular hut as a
centre for his spiritual work. An Army Commander, addressing a conference of chaplains,
laid great stress upon the importance of the
work which the chaplain is able to do in centres such as these, in giving to the men that
encouragement and inspiration without which

so much of their military effectiveness would be lost.

" I am glad," said the King, in a letter written to Sir Douglas Haig this summer after his return from a visit to the Front, " to find that the Army Commanders appreciate the importance of affording means for the amusement and diversion of the troops in their leisure time, and that every effort to this end is undertaken by the authorities and by private help."

No small part of the help here referred to by the King is given by the Church Army.

The men are constantly debating such questions as " Why does God allow the War ? " and " What has Christianity to say to it ? " The chaplains can do a work of real service in showing men that in fighting their country's battles they are at the same time engaged in the fight for righteousness. Many a sermon of this kind has been preached by the chaplains in the Church Army huts, and many a soldier has been strength-

ened to go out and fight his battle in the conviction thus gained that his cause is the cause of
righteousness, and that therefore it must in-
evitably prevail.

It may safely be said that the high spirits
and splendid cheerfulness of our soldiers in
the face of extraordinary difficulties and
constant hardships is due in no small measure
to the refreshment and recreation and encouragement and inspiration which have been received
in such centres of life and activity as our Church
Army huts.   It is good to see the eagerness with
which a battalion, newly arrived in billets, re-
ceives the news that there is a hut in the village.
There is little waiting about when the men are
dismissed ; they make a bee-line for the hut.
And with a sigh of content they throw themselves down on the welcome bench, wearied
after a long march, their mug of tea on the
table in front of them, a packet of fags to smoke
in rapid succession, and an odd assortment of
magazines to read.   There they write their

letters home to sweetheart or wife or mother. For, tired as they are, they are never too tired to keep up the tie that unites them with the dear ones at home.

AT THE BASE

CHAPTER III

AT each of the Channel ports which form the base of British military operations, Church Army Institutions of all kinds are to be found. There are clubs, huts, institutes, and coffee shops at railway stations, on the quays and centres of traffic, in hospital compounds, and indeed wherever our men are accustomed to congregate. Large numbers of men are necessarily required for the Base establishment. They are mostly the older men, or men belonging to the lower categories. Some of them have been wounded at the front, and are now rated as P.B. or P.U., mysterious Army initials meaning respectively "Permanent Base" and "Permanently Unfit."

A Channel port is obviously not an ideal place

for the British Tommy who is seeking to fill up
his hours of recreation. Hence it is that our
huts in these places have a special value; and
particularly valuable is the fact that the huts at
the Base are staffed by ladies.

It will be readily understood that one of the
greatest cravings of our men in France is for
women's society. It is the lack of this which
has caused one of the gravest difficulties of discipline. The men feel it an immense privilege
that they are able to come into the huts and talk
to the ladies who are there to serve them.
Incidentally it may be remarked that never did
the Government take a wiser step in the interests
of the discipline and morality of our men than
when the W.A.A.C.'s were brought out to France,
and allowed to associate with the soldiers.
Officers of high authority have remarked that
this one step has made an immense difference in
smoothing away difficulties of discipline.

The W.A.A.C.'s have not been forgotten by
the Church Army. Clubs have been provided

HUT IN THE COURTYARD OF A FRENCH CHÂTEAU, SHELLED DURING THE GERMAN PUSH OF APRIL 1918, AND REOPENED A FORTNIGHT LATER AFTER REPAIRS.

for them in the principal centres of their work. In a certain town at the Base, a lady in charge of a Soldiers' Club arranged for a large municipal room to be taken for a social, to which the members of the Club were able to invite their young ladies of the W.A.A.C.'s. The canteens of the huts and the French *pâtisseries* were ransacked to provide an unprecedented spread of such luxuries as were obtainable, and throughout the evening the fun was fast and continuous.

" You see, miss, we liked it because it was so select," was the comment of a sergeant-major when the evening was over. The A.C.G. of the Base was present at the social, and, in escorting home afterwards the lady who had organised it, he remarked, " Well, Mrs. D., that was an heroic stunt of yours. It does no end of good to the men to have entertainments of this kind provided for them."

The devoted work which the ladies do in our Base Institutes is beyond praise. They pathetically remark that it is impossible to keep them-

3

selves clean. "Ah," said one with a sigh, "Now I can sympathise with Jane." Jane, it appears, was the between-maid in the lady's house at home, and Jane never seemed able to appear without dirty collar, or dirty apron, or dirty hands. Probably when this lady gets home, Jane will find her shortcomings viewed with more lenient eyes!

Our men value immensely the sympathy which they know they never fail to find in the huts when they need it. A soldier, quite a young lad, was sitting at the table trying to write a letter home. He was alone and miserable, he said, and had just come back from England, where he had been to his mother's funeral. He had a long talk with the lady in the hut, and then in the evening he came back and said, "It has made all the difference to me to have had some one to talk to; you have made me quite cheerful and happy again."

It is not surprising that whenever ladies are in charge of a hut, they should find that the soldiers who come in are always ready to offer their services to help. Once, during a rush there had been a great demand for plates and cups, and these were suddenly found to be exhausted. A volunteer was called for to collect them. He presently appeared with a pile of these precious commodities in his arms, stretching from his waist to his chin. The lady in charge was horrified as she saw him threading his way through the crowd laden in this way. She expected to see the whole of the crockery crash in one fell swoop to the ground. The soldier noticed her look of consternation, and said with a reassuring smile, "Oh, you needn't worry, ma'am, it is nothing to me; you see, I was a waiter in London before the war!"

Men at the Base whose supplies of pay come in regularly seem to have more money than they know how to spend. This especially applies to the Canadians, Australians, and Americans. "A box of matches, please, ma'am," said an American sailor, as he came up to the counter and threw down a twenty-franc note. The lady in charge was short of change and said, "Haven't you a halfpenny?" "No," he answered; then felt in his pocket and produced a franc. He picked up the box of matches, leaving the whole twenty-one francs on the counter. The lady, who in the meantime was striving to collect ninety-five centimes from her till, saw him disappearing and called after him. "Oh, never mind," he said; "that's all right. It doesn't matter about the money so long as I get the matches." Perhaps twenty-one francs for a box of matches is a record, even in the high prices of the war!

Sometimes, on the other hand, a lad will come into the huts absolutely "on the rocks." For some reason or another he has no money at all. To one such boy, who was in great difficulties, the lady superintendent of the hut lent five francs, which the soldier promised to refund as soon as he received his next pay. Weeks went by, and he didn't appear again. But after something like a month he turned up one evening in the hut.

" Where," he asked, " is the lady who was in charge of the hut a month ago ? She lent me five francs when I was in great difficulties, and now I want to pay her back."

It appeared that the very next day he had been suddenly called up to the Front and had had no opportunity till then of discharging his debt.

A large proportion of the soldiers at the Base are elderly men who have not the necessary physique for the Front. A veteran who had been all through the war from the beginning, and had now become a servant in an officers' mess, made great friends with the ladies in the hut.

" One of the drawbacks to being away for so long," he told them, " is that everything changes at home in the meantime. There is my daughter Mary ; she was at school when I left ; and she has just become engaged to a whipper-snapper of a second-lieutenant in the Flying Corps, who would hardly have dared to speak to me when I was at home. And now, if he comes here, I shall have to wait on my own son-in-law in the

mess! Oh, these 'one-star artists,' what airs
they give themselves! And they are only school-
boys, after all!"

The Mons veteran finds it very difficult to
believe in the merits of the new army and its
junior recruits!

Another valuable field of work for the Church
Army at the Base is to be found in the hospitals.
It is a great boon for the hospital patients, when
they begin to progress towards convalescence,
to be able to find recreation and amusement in
the Church Army huts. How they long to
get home again!

Some of the Base hospitals have the reputa-
tion of being for cases which it is unnecessary to
send home. Rightly or wrongly, there is wide-
spread conviction that those who go into hospital
at Z. will never get back to "Blighty." A wounded
Tommy had been brought into a certain Casualty
Clearing Station behind the Front, preparatory
to being sent down to the Base. "Hullo," said a
friend of his, an R.A.M.C. orderly of the hospital

who recognised him, "they will probably send you to Z., and if they do, they will just keep you there until you are well enough to fight again, and then you will go straight back to your regiment." This was not precisely encouraging to Private Smith. Presently the doctor came round, examining each case, and wrote out for each a label describing his condition and stating his destination. Private Smith looked at his card when the Medical Officer had gone away, and sure enough it was to Z. that he was to go !

He at once began to scheme how he could avoid his fate. The train to Z. was to leave at 8 o'clock that evening, but shortly before the time when the orderlies would come round to collect the patients for the train, he slipped out of bed and got underneath. It wasn't an easy thing to do, and the movement caused him excruciating pain owing to the wound in his leg. However, that didn't trouble him, if by this means he could manage to get to England.

The orderlies came round in due course, marking off the names on their list of the wounded as they took them from their beds and placed them on stretchers to carry them to the hospital train. They came to the bed of Private Smith and found it empty. Where could the patient have gone? A hue and cry was raised, but the search was in vain. The train was detained a quarter of an hour behind its scheduled time in order that Private Smith might be found. There was no trace of him. He had most mysteriously disappeared. And finally the train was sent off, leaving him behind.

Private Smith then struggled from underneath, and with great pain and difficulty scrambled back into bed. Presently the head orderly came along and stopped in indignant surprise in front of the bed. With a remarkable exuberance of language and variety of epithet he inquired of Private Smith what he had been doing and where he had been.

" You were to have gone down in the train to Z., and now you have been left behind. I shall have to send you by the train at 7 o'clock to-morrow morning down to Boulogne."

Private Smith did his best to conceal his satisfaction, and the next morning he was carried on board the train. He was taken to Boulogne, and straight on board a hospital ship which carried him over to England.

" Ah," he said to himself, " to think of those other poor chaps being kept for months at Z., and here am I in a hospital at home ! "

The military authorities will not allow ladies to work in the recreation huts except on " Lines of Communication " and at the Base. It is through no fault of the ladies themselves that they have not been allowed to go to the Front. They have begged to be sent there. And it would have added immensely to the value of our Front huts if the request could have been granted.

I do not suggest that it would have been right to allow ladies to go close up to the line ; but there are many districts in the front zone of the armies where their presence might well have been permitted and would have been a boon beyond price. English nurses are employed in the Casualty Clearing Stations at the Front. And where ladies can go as nurses, it would seem that they might equally go as workers in the huts.

Very splendid has been the work which these nurses have done in the up-country field hospitals.

A lady in a hut at the Base, talking to a group of soldiers, asked them what was the finest thing they had seen in the war. They thought for a moment, and then one of them replied with this story :

" Well, ma'am, the grandest thing I have seen out here was this. It happened in the early days of the Boche offensive. There was a C.C.S. in the line of attack and the Boche was only a few miles away. The roads were all choked up with our retreating transport. An officer came in and said, ' C.O.'s orders ; we were to evacuate at once ; the nurses were to leave ; it wasn't possible to get the wounded away ; very sorry, but it couldn't be helped.' Well,

the nurses absolutely refused to go. They said,
' We won't leave the wounded ; if they must be
left behind, we will stay too.' Then the Colonel
came in, and he cursed and swore and threatened.
But all to no purpose, though he got red in the
face. The nurses wouldn't budge.

"Then some one said : ' Well, why not try
to evacuate the wounded ? ' And we set to work.
There were no ambulances at hand, but we
managed to rake up all sorts of odd shacks on
wheels and we got the men on board. And some
we carried. And the Sisters worked like heroes
to help. And we got every one of them away,
And then a shell came over and laid the big
canvas ward flat! But thanks to those women
every one was safe. And that is the finest thing
I have seen in the war."

ON L. OF C.

CHAPTER IV

ON L. OF C.

WE are to make our journey by the lines of communication up to the Front. The journey will be a slow one, as the train drags itself along at the lowest possible pace; but it will never be dull, for there is so much to see. We shall pass innumerable scenes of activity and preparation of every kind. At various points on the lines there are huge accumulations of forage waiting for distribution. Here and there we shall pass a number of " tanks " waiting by the roadside ready to be entrained. We may see a huge motor repair establishment, where broken-down cars of every description are being refitted so as to be sent up again to the Front. Large numbers of men, therefore, are required at various points on L. of C. (Lines of Communication). These men also require provision made for their recreation and rest, and among them the Church Army has found a fruitful field for its work.

Let us pay a visit, for instance, to a beautiful mediæval town which for our present purpose we may call St. Jacques. It was in this town that I had the privilege of working in the summer of 1917. Before the war this was a sleepy old cathedral town, which became half awake every Saturday to run a market, and wholly awake every religious festival, and then went to sleep again till the next market-day or intervening *Jours des Fêtes*. But now it is all bustle. The streets are not wide enough for the traffic that throngs them. Some streets are closed altogether to wheeled traffic to allow the pedestrians a chance to get through. One such narrow alley has been nicknamed the " Dardanelles "! and is the fashionable rendezvous for Tommy out for a stroll after his work is over.

The cathedral is very beautiful, and the people make it, in a very real way, their home. One can never go into it without finding many worshippers kneeling in silent prayer. There are mothers and daughters praying for their *poilus* at the Front; there are many in black, and it is easy to guess what is the subject of their prayers. Indeed, there are very many families in France that have a dear one to mourn.

My own hut was not far from the station. And a very busy station it is, with many huge troop-trains coming and going. Indeed, the trains are so long that one is surprised that the engine is able to move them at all. Perhaps the weight of the trains accounts for the interminable length of a railway journey in France in war-time. The train goes so slowly that one feels inclined to get out and push behind.

We lesser fry look with envy at the " brass hats " and red-banded staff officers, who dodge about everywhere in gorgeous motors at forty miles an hour ! The train goes by fits and starts,

4

sometimes stopping for an hour at a time, pre-
ferably just outside a station, tantalisingly out
of reach of the refreshments, which are eagerly
looked for after a ten or fifteen hours' journey!
However, the trains do sometimes stop in the
station; and if it happens to be our station, and
the officers are considerate and military exigencies
allow, we get a rush of soldiers into the hut and
are kept busy dealing out tea and bread-and-
butter and other delights at top speed. And
what a tremendous demand for cigarettes!
Pipes appear to be entirely at a discount with
the British Tommy nowadays, unless it is an
N.C.O. of the " Old Contemptibles," who comes
in to get his ounce of shag. One day it will be
Canadians, another day Australians; occasionally we have a rush of stalwart Americans,
besieging the canteen and waving dollar-notes
in our faces, and all claiming to be served at
once as their train is going in two minutes'
time. Like a thunderstorm, the " push " is
short and sharp; presently the engine whistles

and the men bolt back to their train.   In a few days' time, perhaps, they are in the front line of trenches;   who knows ?

I had not been many days at St. Jacques when I was hailed with the question, " How is Rotherhithe getting on ! " I looked up and saw a face with a broad grin—a friend from the old parish!   Indeed I have met many friends in khaki from the riverside and the docks.   " Hullo, Mr. Durell, who'd have thought to meet you here ? " was a greeting I received as I came out of the Town Major's office.   It is good to meet the lads from " Blighty," and they love to be reminded of the old church and the home that is so often in their thoughts.   That is part, at least, of what the parson stands for in their eyes.

Occasionally men were detrained here to be marched up to the trenches, so it was necessary to keep the hut open all night in order to give hot coffee and rolls to the men when they left the train.   It was a weird sensation—those nights in the hut.   The lights carefully veiled and pitch darkness outside ; in the distance the constant booming of guns, which never ceased ; and presently the arrival of the troop-train in the darkened station. We were told to be ready to put out our lights at a moment's notice, as " Taubes " were said to be about.

When the train came in I went to the station and groped around till I found the commanding officer, and told him that we had a Church Army hut open near the station, and that we would welcome his men if he cared to bring them in for some food before marching them away. It is delightful to see how gratefully such an offer as this is accepted ; and still more delightful to see the gratitude of the men, when they come in stiff and weary after their long monotonous journey through the night, and get set up with food and hot drinks for their tedious march out to camp.

It is a strenuous time serving hundreds upon hundreds of hungry men, who fill the hut in relays. Behind the counter are three parsons in their shirt sleeves and the then Chief Commissioner of the Church Army, who had come to lend a hand for the occasion; in the background are the orderlies, working the urns and keeping the water boiling.

So we toil and perspire through the hours of the night. And it is well worth it. The men will march all the better for what we have been able to do for them. And they will perhaps take away with them a picture in their minds—a group of parsons who. are happy to roll up their shirt sleeves and do something for Tommy's comfort in the middle of the night.

It will help them to realise that the Church is out to help them. And I cannot but feel that, though in such a hut as this there was little opportunity for the holding of services, yet the indirect spiritual influence of the hut, from the mere presence of the clergy in it, was very real. I am convinced that a parson is able to do true spiritual work in these Church Army huts. He is brought into closer contact

with the men than the official Chaplains to the
Forces are always able to obtain. For the
chaplain is handicapped at the start by his
position as an officer, which necessarily sets him
apart from the men. This barrier can be broken
down, and is broken down. But it takes a
real man to do it. And unless the chaplain is a
man, the handicap is too great for him, and he
fails. But the chaplains out here are a splendid
set of men, and have done magnificently. I
know a D.A.C.G. who wrote up on the door of
his billet, "Abandon rank, all ye who enter
here!" It is only here and there that one comes
across the *petit maître*, who reminds you that he
is an officer, and is always looking out for salutes.
Such a one is of course worse than useless as a
representative of the Church at the Front.

The work in the Church Army hut provides a
splendid opportunity for clergy who are unable
to leave their parishes for the whole year required
of a Chaplain to the Forces, but are able to give
the four months which is the minimum that

military regulations allow. There is no doubt that the presence of priests as managers of a hut does really create a cleaner atmosphere, and is a reminder of the claims of religion.

It is a pleasure to see the delightful manners of the men in the hut, and to witness their gratitude for what we try to do for them. Especially conspicuous is the considerateness of those who have seen the real thing in the front trenches, who have been " over the top " and in many a tight place in the fighting line. There is an obvious difference between such men and those who have only been engaged in " cushy " jobs on the lines of communication or at the Base. The behaviour in the hut is always the behaviour of gentlemen. And the British soldier in France is a real gentleman. If ever, by some unusual chance, the language in the hut becomes what it should not be, a quiet word is all that is needed to prevent a recurrence.

The town of St. Jacques was always full of interest. Sometimes aircraft paid us a visit at night, and we were awakened by the warning clang of the cathedral bell, followed quickly by the firing of the "Archies." Immediately opposite to my billet was a Girls' Orphanage under the care of Sisters. Whenever an air-raid was on, these little girls all began to pray out loud in chorus, and we heard their voices across the street.

In the early morning I was generally awakened by a heavy tramp beneath my windows. It was a gang of German prisoners going to work under the charge of an armed guard. Presently another gang followed, and then another. These men mostly had a hang-dog look ; they marched with their eyes on the ground. But they were exceedingly well cared for ; and if our prisoners were half as well looked after by the enemy as these are by us, one of the deepest tragedies of the war would be removed.

I was waited on in my billet by an old French veteran who had fought at Sedan in 1870—a dear old man, who looks now to see France set free from the dark cloud that has been over her since the Franco-Prussian War. He is an old inhabitant of St. Jacques. His most cherished possession was a beautiful fifteenth-century figure of the Blessed Virgin, holding in her arms the Holy Child. This, together with other of his heirlooms, he was accustomed to show me with special pride. In a recent bombardment of the town his house has been completely destroyed. The only thing in it that escaped destruction was this figure of the Blessed Virgin. It was protected by a heavy table, which was hurled across the room by the force of the explosion, and formed a protective barrier in front of this priceless work of art. On the same night the Girls' Orphanage was destroyed by a bomb, which fortunately did not penetrate into the cellar in which the children were gathered together; so that a terrible loss of life was avoided.

Sometimes, as we came away from the hut at night, tired out after a long day's work, we would see a sudden light flare up in the east.

Something big was going on where the armies were facing one another across No Man's Land. And always there was the distant booming of the guns. And we wondered what would be to-morrow's news.

BEHIND THE TRENCHES

CHAPTER V

BEHIND THE TRENCHES

A CHURCH ARMY COMMISSIONER in the Front
areas in France has an opportunity, such as is
given perhaps to few, of seeing on a broad scale
what is being done for the welfare of the troops
behind our lines. For it is his business to speed
in his car over the whole of the Army area to
which he is attached, visiting the Church Army
huts and examining their needs with a view
to securing from the appropriate military
authority that help which is always so generously
given when called for, and without which our
huts could not be run for a single day.

Thus, in the performance of his duties, not
only does the Church Army Commissioner see
what his own huts are doing for the men, but

also he is brought into contact with the high officials of the Army in its various departments, and so has the opportunity of learning how the whole subject of the welfare of the men is being tackled on the Western Front. And it is impossible not to be struck by the anxiety that is everywhere shown that nothing should be left undone that makes for the greater comfort and happiness and well-being of our soldiers.

There is in every army or corps or division a mysterious individual known as " Q." The initial almost seems to suggest something connected with the High Criticism. However, there is nothing destructive about " Q." He is, in fact, a means of construction, the source from which issue such things as material and labour and transport. These are things of which the Church Army huts stand in constant need, and the commissioner who wants to get a floor relaid or a leaky roof renewed or a broken stove repaired has to solicit the interest and seek the help of " Q."

Timber may be difficult to get and labour may be scarce, but if the thing can be done our friends at court may be trusted to do it. They tell us that they are all out to help the Church Army, and by their actions they prove that their assertion is true.

But why should they do so? Why, amid all the absorbing problems of the war, should busy men at Head-quarters give time and thought to our work? Come into a Church Army hut one evening in the short winter days and you will find for yourself the answer to this question.

Externally the hut is a strange-looking creature. Its sides spread out laterally instead of rising vertically from the ground. The purpose of this is to enable it to combine maximum strength with minimum weight. This is necessary, because sometimes the hut has to be picked up and set down elsewhere in order to follow military movements. But it gives the hut something of the appearance of an unwieldy reptile squatting on the ground.

Suppose, then, that the hour is about 5.30 p.m. We stumble through the dark by the aid of an electric torch, absolutely indispensable if we do not want to measure our length in a sea of mud.   We pick our way along the trench ladders which lead through the swamp up to the door. Inside the hut all is brightness and animation. At one end the canteen is hard at work dealing out tea, biscuits, cigarettes, and other objects of luxury.   The tables are crowded with men writing letters home, or playing games. Very probably we shall find a parson in charge.

"Now, lads, get ready for the concert," is the order given. The tables are put away; forms and chairs are set out in rows. It is to be a great occasion, for the star Pierrot Party of the corps is to perform. The corps are very proud of their concert troupe, and well they may be, for the greater part of the best male music-hall talent of London is on the Western Front, and is enlisted in the various divisional or corps parties whose function it is to provide amuse-

HUT OVERLOOKING THE VALLEY OF THE RIVER ———, AN IMPORTANT STRATEGIC LINE IN THE GERMAN OFFENSIVE OF APRIL 1918.

ment for the men. And it is the boast of the corps that never a word is heard in the programmes of their troupe to which the most fastidious could object.

Presently the corps lorry arrives, and a number of mysterious packages are carried from it into the hut by lads in khaki, who in a few minutes will appear as Pierrots and Pierrettes on the stage. Next there arrive a couple of cars from corps head-quarters, bringing " brass hats " and other red- or blue-banded personages who are decorously received by the superintendent and ushered into the front seats. For the high military authorities show by their presence, as well as by their ever-ready help, their appreciation of the work which the huts are doing for the men.

The concert begins, and soon the house is rocking with laughter at the jokes and facial contortions of the funny man of the party, or joining at the top of their voices in the chorus of some well-known song. Allusions to Tommy's

5

attempts at the French language, or to Fritz's delicate attentions in the matter of shells dropped over the line, never fail to elicit roars of laughter.

The " lady in the case " is played by one of the less stalwart members of the caste, and these impersonations are little short of marvellous. Wonderful hats are ordered from Paris for the " leading lady," regardless of expense ; and the " Little Bit of Fluff " in the centre of the stage is almost as charming and delightful as the genuine article could be !

A troupe of Pierrots from a newly arrived division once came to play in the principal theatre in our country town behind the lines. After the performance the stage door was beseiged by quite a crowd of officers, all eager for the honour of escorting the " lady " to her hotel. So perfectly feminine and fascinating had been the impersonation that they were convinced that the old 999th had imported a French lady into the caste. They were sadly disillusioned when the "O.C. Troupe" came out and they recognised his features!

In the sarcasm and witticisms of the dialogue in these variety entertainments we often find reflections of various popular ideas or superstitions current in the Army. They throw sidelights upon what the men are thinking.

There is, for instance, an impression current that "Signals," the branch of the service that deals with telephones, telegraphs, and messages of every kind, are specially favoured by that particular Providence that watches over comforts and privileges. So on our Variety Stage Private Wangle appears as an awkward recruit in a very awkward squad. He is wearing on his arm the blue and white brassard distinctive of "Signals." The drill sergeant is furious.

"Why are you wearing that blinking band?" he shouts. "Take the blarsted thing off at once."

Private Wangle looks up innocently, and answers: "I put it on because they told me that, if I did, I should get the best billet in the town."

Army signals are very cruel to the alphabet. It is difficult to distinguish sounds sometimes on a field telephone, and words often have to be spelt out, letter by letter. But A, B, C, D, are liable to confusion; so the poor letters appear under the disguise of Ack, Beer, Cee, Don, and so on. Nor is this sufficient. To avoid calamitous mistakes the identity of the letter has to be further established by reference to a word of which it is the initial.

Thus one hears this kind of thing from an operator who has to call up the siege artillery and is trying to convey the word "Heavies" to the other end of the line by laboriously spelling it out. "Hullo, Siege Park, are you there? H for Home; no, Home, H O M E (a sustained crescendo)—H O M E—the place where you would like to be"; and at last, losing his temper, "Very well, then, H for ——; and you'd better go there too."

Confusion now is worse confounded, for the receiver at the other end is now firmly convinced that the word in question begins with L ! Ah, the tackling of a field telephone is a glorious lesson in patience !

One raises no objection to such elucidations as " C for Charlie, F for Freddy, H for Home." But when it comes to transmitting the letters B, S, M, K by calling through the telephone " Beer for Bertie, Essays for Susan, Emma for Mary, Kisses for Kate," one feels that the limits of literary licence have been reached.

This, however, is a digression. Our concert in the hut runs through its successive phases from grave to gay. At 7.30 p.m. it is all over, for we keep early hours at the Front. We all stand for " The King," the " brass hats " file out, Columbine reappears in khaki, and by eight o'clock the hut is closed for the night.

TOMMY'S RELIGION

CHAPTER VI

TOMMY'S RELIGION

WE have seen something of a Church Army hut in its lighter moments. Now come to this same hut on a Sunday evening. The canteen is closed and the hut is filled with men who have come for a voluntary service.

The chaplains find a special opportunity in these voluntary services which are always held in our huts on Sunday evenings. The morning parades have necessarily an official character, which is entirely absent from the evening service. Everything is done to make it clear that no one need join in this service unless he wishes to do so. A certain number of tables for writing and reading are always left undisturbed at the end of the hut away from the stage, where the altar

77

has been erected and from which the service is taken. All who desire to do so are able to go on with their previous occupations while the service is being held.

The great majority, however, prefer to leave their reading and to sit on the cross benches where they can take part in the service. And very inspiring these voluntary services are. Every man who is there is present because he means it. And how they love to sing the hymns! And they love the canticles, too. Experience shows that a liturgical service on the lines of Evensong, with responses and canticles sung, with the Lord's Prayer and Creed intoned, and with the proper collects duly said, is much more appreciated than an inorganic sing-song of the kind that men are popularly supposed to love.

" You see, sir," a man said to me, " it reminds us of the old parish church at home, and that is why we like it."

But there is something still more sacred in the little chapel which, whenever possible, is attached to a Church Army hut. In the beautiful chapel belonging to the hut, to which its anonymous donor gave the name of " Good Friend "—a name it has splendidly earned—the Holy Communion is celebrated daily. Of course, not many of the rank and file can ever attend this service on account of their military duties; but, as the preacher said at a Sunday evening service in the hut, " We want you to know that when you are on parade outside your chaplains are also on parade at God's Altar, and are offering their prayers for you and for our dear ones at home."

In this chapel the Blessed Sacrament is always reserved, so that at any hour of the day or night, when the hut is open, men may receive their Communion before going up to the trenches. They will come to the chaplain in all their heavy marching kit in little groups of four or five.

" Sir, we are going up to the line in an hour's time. May we take Communion before we go ? "

And so, after a short Communion office in that little chapel, the Bread of Life is administered to the kneeling group. And they go forth all the stronger and happier to meet the unknown dangers and sufferings that lie before them in the line.

It constantly falls to my lot to take the services in one or other of our Church Army huts; sometimes the parade service in the morning, sometimes the voluntary service in the evening. The services, of course, are all arranged by the chaplains, but the Chaplains' Department was till recently so far below its proper strength that it was quite impossible for the chaplains to take all the services that were required, if the needs of the men were to be adequately met. It is of the utmost importance that the Chaplains' Department should be kept up to strength.

There is something very inspiring about our services at the Front, and something also very suggestive. For at the Front we have a freer hand than is possible in parish churches at home, and we can make experiments. Our task is to ascertain how best we can meet the needs of " Tommy " ; and " Tommy," in this war of nations, means the average Englishman. Any light, therefore, which the experience of the Front throws upon this problem will be of direct value in guiding those far-reaching changes which will have to be made in the methods of the Church at home if she is to win something of her rightful place in the nation when the men return after the war.

One fact which has emerged is the strong appeal made to the men by a service in which they know how to take an active part and in which they are encouraged to do so. I have in my mind conspicuously a parade service which I took on the fourth Sunday in Advent. A large building, once apparently the public hall of the village, but now annexed by the military, was packed with men from end to end. The battalion had only just come into rest from the trenches, and there was still some uncertainty as to where various articles of equipment were to be found. At the last moment it was discovered that there were no books of any sort available for the men. What was to be done? Although Christmas was still two days ahead, we decided to anticipate the Church season, and to sing the Christmas hymns, in the hope that the men would know them by heart. And how they sang! On the platform was the drum-and-fife band of the battalion. The drums were piled in front for my benefit, and then, without any printed music, the fifes accompanied us as we sang, " O come, all ye faithful," " Hark, the herald angels sing," and " While shepherds watched their flocks by night." After the service the C.O. came to me and said, " Why should we ever have books at a parade service again? I have never heard the men sing like that before ! "

I shall not easily forget a parade service which I took at Easter for a Balloon Section not far from A——. On a clear day one ran the risk of being met at the ground by the apology,

" Very sorry, Padre, but this is a splendid morning for observation, and the old ' sausage ' has got to go up at once; so all our men must turn out, and a Church Parade is impossible."

However, on this Easter morning a blue haze blotted out the distant landmarks and the degree of visibility was very low, so I had no fear of my parade being " off."

I was welcomed at the mess by the C.O., hardly more than a boy, in spite of the major's crown on his arm. He might have been a fresher at the 'Varsity; but then, youth is the badge of all branches of the Royal Air Force. A man mustn't be too old, if he has to be prepared to jump at a moment's notice out of a balloon at a height of a thousand feet from the ground !

" Hullo, Padre ! Good luck to you ! " was the greeting I received. " Come along into the mess and get your things on ! We are all ready for the parade."

Near by, the big yellow " sausage " balloon was pinned down to the ground, ready inflated, so that as soon as visibility improved it might ascend without loss of time.

The hymns had been selected by the sergeant-major, who presided at the piano. A soldier's choice of hymns is an indication of his outlook on religion; and it is interesting from this point of view to note the hymns that are popular favourites. It is often our custom on Sunday evenings, instead of beginning the voluntary hut service exactly at the advertised time, to sing a number of preliminary hymns sitting, while the congregation, with varying degrees of unpunctuality, are gradually assembling. The men are invited to call for a favourite hymn, and then a verse or two—perhaps the first and last—are sung.

There is no lack of competition among the men to secure a turn for their own special favourite. And this fifteen-minute sing-song allows us to see clearly what kind of hymns the men like to sing. They are strangely fond of such hymns as " Jerusalem the Golden "—per-

CHAPEL OF A HUT NEAR THE FRONT.

haps they like the contrast it suggests to their
own drab existence in the mud of northern
France!—but I suppose the prime favourite of
all is,

> "Holy Father, in Thy mercy,
>   Hear our anxious prayer:
>   Keep our loved ones, now far absent,
>   'Neath Thy care."

It takes the exile's thoughts back to his home
across the sea.

The sergeant-major of my Balloon Section
handed me the list of hymns he had chosen.
It was a little bit surprising to find " There
is a green hill far away" among the hymns he
had put down for Easter Day! But it didn't
really matter, as the Easter message could be
kept for the sermon.

And how extraordinarily the Easter message
out in France this year seemed to fit in with all
that was uppermost in our minds! Remember
that these were the early days of the tremendous
offensive on the Somme. From an outsider's

6

point of view, the prospect looked dark, and we wondered how far the retreat would go.

Then came the festival of Easter, with its message of a victory won through the agony of the Cross, through suffering, tragedy, and death. We saw the wounded coming back from the battlefield; we knew of those others lying dead on the ground. And we thought of it as the crucifixion of our country on the terrible cross of war. But Easter spoke to us of the certainty that, through this frightful crucifixion in the struggle against the dark forces of materialism and evil, there would come a new life. An Easter victory must be ours, as right must triumph over wrong, and a new and better and happier England would rise to a new life from this horror and welter of death.

I had the opportunity after the service of talking to one of the N.C.O.'s. He said that many a man had been led by the war to look beyond this life and to think of deeper things. I believe that this is true; and I believe that the message of

Good Friday and of Easter went home to many a heart at the Front this year.

It has been said that any religion that has been stirred in the men by the war has been merely a religion of fear. It has been induced by the fear of death on the eve of a battle or before going " over the top," and it evaporates as soon as the fear which evoked it has passed.

There may be something in this criticism; but I am convinced that it presents a partial view. I am sure that there is much more in the soldier's religion than this. There is many a soldier who feels that materialism can never again be supposed to give an adequate account of a universe in which have been exhibited such spiritual qualities of love, self-sacrifice, and heroism as have been everyday experiences amid the horrors of this war.

AT THE FRONT

CHAPTER VII

AT THE FRONT

LET me now take you in imagination close up to the firing line, and show you the Church Army at work in a district under direct observation of the enemy. It is in the centre of the mining country, upon which before the war depended the busy industrial life of North-Eastern France. The place I have in my mind was the model mine of France; its buildings are all quite new, erected on the most approved lines and fitted with the best modern machinery. All around the pithead a great mining village was laid out in the form of a Garden City. It was planned with broad boulevards, by the sides of which stood the miners' cottages, each with a garden of its own. Clearly the mining company were anxious to do all they could for the welfare of

the men and their families. What a contrast
between this and so many of our English pit
villages! It must have been a happy and pros-
perous place, giving a means of livelihood to
some five or six thousand persons.

Now, what a scene of sorrow and desolation!
The large coal elevator is a mass of twisted steel;
the palatial building which housed the offices
of the mine is a wreck.

Let us go and find a ruined house with some
of our British Tommies in possession. They
have built themselves a fireplace, and pushed
up their amateur chimney through an impro-
vised roof. In the house itself not a door or
a banister is to be seen. All woodwork has long
been broken up to "keep the home fires burning."

There is no place or means of recreation within
reach of the men, not even an *estaminet*, for the
entire civil population has been evacuated from
the neighbourhood; and you cannot, of course,
play football within sight of the enemy observers!
So the Church Army has literally and metaphoric-

ally stepped into the breach. Steer your way with me carefully round the shell-holes in the ground to the roofless building which was once the business centre of the mine. You wear your " tin hat," and your box respirator must be at hand, ready to fix on at a moment's notice. For Fritz has a playful habit of " putting a few over," if he happens to think of it, and so we have to be prepared.

Life in this place never lacks excitement. In its neighbourhood a series of captive balloons keep up incessant observation, whenever the air is clear, of all that is going on behind the German lines. One afternoon we heard a special fury of firing suddenly burst out, and we ran out to see what kind of stunt was on. A Boche plane was overheard, flying very swiftly and very high. The Archies were pursuing him with their fire. Little balls of white fluff kept forming in the blue sky ; these were bursting shrapnel.

But it was not easy to get the range all at once, and the Boche did all he could to disconcert the gunners by rapid manœuvres. We soon saw what game he was after, for he made a sudden swoop downwards to the level of the nearest " sausage," circled round it and fired his machine gun into its bulk.

A little spot of dull red showed up against the surface of the balloon in the sunshine. A cry went up from the eagerly watching spectators: " He's got it ! " And in a few seconds the whole mass was in flames.

In an instant the observers in the car of the balloon had jumped overboard, and presently, far below, we saw three parachutes opening and descending slowly to the ground. It is a nerve-shaking thing—that jumping from a balloon. Two hundred feet of unimpeded fall, and then the haul back as the parachute opens! But supposing it doesn't open ? It is not surprising if after a jump from a " sausage " the observers have to be sent back into rest.

But our excitement was not yet over. There was another balloon a little farther away. Fearless of the Archies, who threatened at any moment to get his range, the Boche sought his second prey. And he got it, too! And then a third! Each was brought down in flames.

" Well," said an onlooker; " he's about the pluckiest Boche I have seen. He deserves to get away!"

But would he? He was evidently winged. His engine had stopped and he was swaying unsteadily. There was something amiss with his controls. But he had nearly got out of range of the Archies, and he was not far from his own lines. Lower and lower he came as he neared the German trenches. He was almost within rifle range from our front line. The machine seemed to rock dangerously, but he kept his balance and reached his home. And so strong is the sporting instinct in our men that I really believe that the little group who had breathlessly watched the flight were glad that the Boche had escaped.

The excitement was over, and we went back to smoke our cigarettes and to drink our tea.

Changes and movements at the Front are constantly bringing new openings, which the Church Army is asked to fill. A new Corps comes into an area and has new ideas as to centres to be selected for billeting; or the centre of gravity of the strategic position changes and new encampments spring into existence.

In the course of such movements a certain village not many miles behind the trenches seemed likely to become what military strategists describe as a " nodal point " and we anticipated that it would shortly be crowded out with troops.

The D.A.C.G. of the Corps was anxious that we should provide a hut for his men in this desolate village. It stood in complete isolation in the midst of a network of canals and ditches in the bleak fen country, and the men would have very little to give them comfort or recreation beyond what we might be able to supply.

So we enlisted the services of the Sub-Area

Commandant, with a view to securing a site for a hut.

" Church Army hut ? " he said ; " yes, certainly, there's a field bang in the middle of the village—suit you excellently. Come and see it."

This was cheering, and we started on our tour of inspection. A very muddy opening between two tumbledown houses, just opposite the ruined church, led into a field behind the village street. The opening was decorated with a notice board bearing the ominous words : " To the Incinerator."

Now the student of the Front is accustomed to give the local incinerator a wide berth, just as he is wont to avoid too close contact with the fatigue parties who for large extra pay work those horrible French machines which pump the sewage out of the cesspools of town houses through monstrous pipes laid along the central passage and out at the front door.

So we looked rather askance at the kiln-like erection across the field, to which all the refuse of the village had to be brought to be destroyed by slow combustion. A heavy pall of smoke hung above it, for combustion was far from complete, and there was no Borough Council at hand to compel the machine to consume its own smoke.

The Sub-Area Commandant noticed our glance of dismay and tried to reassure us.

"It won't matter much," he said. "The smoke will generally blow the other way. And you can build the hut end on to the Incinerator, so that even if the wind should happen to lie in this direction, the smoke will almost always miss the hut."

It seemed rather like suggesting to a merchant ship to be careful to keep end on to a submarine, so as to give it the smallest possible mark for a torpedo. It would appear preferable to keep out of the way altogether!

So we gently hinted to our friend that the neighbourhood of an Incinerator, however convenient on other grounds, was hardly consistent with the dignity of the Church Army! It seemed possible that if the smoke, so delicately compounded of all sorts of savoury elements, did succeed in getting inside the hut, it might give an unexpected flavour to the tea, which not even the conflicting fumes of innumerable cigarettes would be able to disguise.

So we begged him to look out another site for us, and it was not long before we had our hut pegged out in a field in which there were no rival attractions. This hut, sad to say, had a short life, and not even a merry one. For it was in the area overwhelmed by the German push in the spring, when over a hundred of our Front huts were swept out of existence. We knew, of course, the risk we were taking in placing it so close to the line, but the welfare of the men was our primary consideration. At all costs our lads in these dangerous areas must be given such a measure of comfort and recreation as our huts are able to provide.

Sometimes a country town fairly close to the

line has escaped destruction, and it is possible to turn the palatial residence of some French magnate into an Institute for the men. If the owner has sought safety in Paris or elsewhere, it is generally possible to rent the house through the kind offices of the Town Major.

Such a house we decided to take in a certain town. An Officers' Club had just gone " scat," owing to the removal of a Division to another area, and we bought up all the furniture of the Club so as to have a really top-hole Institute for the men. A room was set apart for use as a chapel and another was placed at the disposal of the D.A.C.G. of the Corps, so that the house might be used as a spiritual centre for the chaplains' work in the Corps area.

But sad to say, the Boche offensive in the spring brought the town under shell-fire. Our beautiful Institute was one day totally destroyed by two direct hits of high-explosive shells, while the superintendent and his two soldier orderlies were at breakfast.

A CHURCH ARMY INSTITUTE IN AN UNHEALTHY AREA.

A PIT HEAD IN NORTHERN FRANCE.

The superintendent tells how the first shells of this offensive fell in the street, in which the house stood, at 4 a.m. that morning. At about 7.30 a.m. a violent explosion in front of the house caused them to go out. Five soldiers were lying about on the ground shockingly injured. One was dead and two others died during the day. The superintendent carried the two who could be moved into the house for safety. He then went some short distance under fire to the Military School to notify the casualties and to obtain ambulances, and finally he saw the men safely away.

He and his staff had returned to breakfast, when a heavy shell fell in the back garden of the house, making a crater fifteen feet deep, shattering the outhouses and shaking the premises at the rear. They then sought refuge in the narrow front hall, that being a strongly supported part of the building. Fifteen minutes later a heavy shell struck the roof and exploded in the house and brought down the entire structure

7

of three floors in a mass of débris. A small part of the ceiling over their heads in the passage withstood the shock and saved their lives ; but the senior orderly was buried to the waist and the superintendent with the second orderly had to dig with their hands for an hour before they were able to liberate him. He was taken to hospital with a crushed foot.

The superintendent went out with the local battalion when they evacuated the town and remained with them by the roadside, while they awaited instructions as to their destination. During the afternoon he remembered the box of soldiers' letters that had stood in the hall of the Institute, waiting to be cleared for the mail. He returned alone into the town, over which shrapnel was exploding in spasmodic bursts. With some difficulty and in considerable danger from the tottering walls and overhanging timbers, he rescued the letters. This visit enabled him to realise how complete was the destruction of the house. The only item of his belongings that he was able to extract from the débris and bring away was a Bible, the gift of his little daughter.

The officer in command of the battalion came along the country road to express his thanks for the help that had been given to his wounded men; and the authorities at Corps head-quarters spoke in very high terms of the way in which the emergency had been met by the staff of this Church Army Institute.

Omelettes, it is said, cannot be made without breaking eggs. Certainly the Church Army work at the Front this year has involved many breakages and heavy loss. But it has been well worth it, for what we have been able to do for the men. And we would lose as many more in the same cause if necessary!

" Oh, you won't have to do that," said one of our lads with a cheery smile, " the tide has turned now, and we shall soon have old Fritz on the run ! "

And the prophecy seems likely to be true. We

are again in occupation of the tortured site of this old mediæval town, once so beautiful and picturesque. It is now merely a heap of ruins from end to end, wantonly destroyed by the Boche before evacuation in a fury of disappointed rage.

THE RUINED COUNTRY

CHAPTER VIII

THE RUINED COUNTRY

IT was my duty to drive each week through the devastated area that lies north of Arras and behind the mining district of Lens. What a scene of ruin and desolation is revealed by this once thriving countryside! Dominating it all are the twin towers of the church of Mont St. Eloi on the highest point of the ridge that runs westward to the once wooded spur of Notre Dame de Lorette.

The ruined church of Mont St. Eloi is a monument to the Prussian infamy of 1870. It was in the Franco-Prussian War of "Soixante-dix" that the church was shelled. Its towers have remained to this day in the condition in which the Prussian gunners left them. They stand aloft on their hill crest, visible as a landmark for miles around. It is curious how their outline varies, as seen from different points of view. Sometimes they appear as a single rocky mass, as though a gigantic Druidic monolith had been erected on the ridge. From other directions the jagged line of the edge shows clear, where successive shells broke away blocks of the masonry at different stages of its height. From yet other points of view the two towers stand out separate from one another, with the torn façade of the church between. The light and shade of sun and cloud play upon their scarred face, and the flowering plants of France have pushed their roots between their stones. Never, perhaps, do the towers look so beautiful as when the setting sun has thrown the hill village at their feet into shadow and the weather-worn stones glow in its level rays.

ow the old ruin of Mont St. Eloi looks

out over a district that is ruin from end to end.

Let us journey from it eastwards to Ablain St. Nazaire, nestling under the shadow of its hills. In a secluded nook, beautiful as some Cistercian Abbey, is its parish church, now, alas! a ruin. The delicate traceries of its windows show up no longer against the dark of its stained glass, but against the blue of the sky. Prussian hate has wreaked its vengeance upon its stones, but in doing so has erected a memorial of that day when the victorious French drove them from the village to the lower ground beyond.

Follow the line of the German retreat, and we come to where Souchez is marked on the map. But Souchez is no longer there. Not even a ruin of its houses remains. We are conscious of having entered the site of the village, for the *pavé* begins in the road. We know when we have left the village behind, for the *pavé* has come to an end. A little stream crosses the road and winds along a twisted course. The very contour of the ground has been changed by the tearing of the shells, and a new channel has been carved out for the stream.

But the sugar refinery of Souchez, which played such a conspicuous part in the victorious battles of the French in this part of the line—where is it ? We look in vain for a building. Not even a blackened wall remains. But presently we find some broken masses of twisted iron. They are all that remains to tell of its existence.

We may follow the main Béthune road northwards to Aix Noulette, and again the same tale of ruin and desolation meets us. The church is but a shell; its vaulted roof lies a shapeless mass upon the ground.

Or we may turn southwards to seek the village of La Targette. We look for it in vain. Equally with Souchez it has absolutely disappeared.

Before the war this countryside was beautifully wooded. Look now at the dead relics of its forests; broken tree-trunks stand up as bare gaunt poles, all cut off by the passage of the shells at varying heights from the ground. A wild, rank vegetation, from which they rise like white ghosts, makes the ground green at their feet.

Old trenches, with sides crumbling away, run by the roadside or across what once were fields. Here and there we find what seems to be a broken tree stump, with jagged top and moss-covered sides. We look more closely, and we see that it is an old, long-disused observation post. It is a hollow case, fashioned to look like a tree of which the top has been cut off by a shell. It has a ladder inside, and a slit for an observer to look out over what was once the German line.

But the Germans have long been pushed back beyond the range of hills that bound our vision in the east. In the distance we see the ruins of the mining suburb of Liévin, and just beyond the brow of the ridge are the towers of Lens.

And that ridge! Famous indeed in the history of the war; for it is Vimy Ridge: a name that will be for ever written in letters of gold in the annals of Canadian prowess. For it was the Canadians who, as all the world knows, pushed the Germans over the ridge to the low ground beyond.

Its sides are seamed by the lines of the old German trenches, where the excavated chalk still shows white against the green of the downs. Here and there, as above the ruined village of Roclincourt, the tumbled masses on the ridge crest mark the site of the explosion of Canadian mines.

From the site of Ecurie, no longer a village, we can look down south, to where in a gap between the folds of the hills we can see the ruined towers of Arras. The cathedral and the Hôtel de Ville are there, each of them a shapeless

IN THE RUINED COUNTRY.   OLD BRITISH TRENCH IN FOREGROUND.

mass. The Town Hall of Arras was one of the
glories of the Renaissance, but what mattered
that to the Hun? As I stood by its ruins
a shell came screaming over and buried itself
in the street behind. It was as though the
impersonated Fury of Germany were shriek-
ing, "Leave sentiment alone. What care I
for art or beauty? Let all perish, so Germany
may rule."

From this ruined country I return to my
quarters when night has fallen. And how eerie
and strange is this country after dark! All
along the Front the Verey lights are being tossed
up into the sky in constant succession, throwing
a strange white light over the landscape. Weird
shadows make uncouth shapes over this wild
scene behind the lines.

Then there are the gun flashes, concealed so
far as may be so that the gun emplacement may
not be discovered by the enemy.

One of our planes will pass over, carrying
its light on its wings; sometimes dropping

red or blue lights, like Roman candles, to give signals which only the initiated can interpret.

Farther back from the line we may find a circle of bright lights on the ground. They mark the limits of an aerodrome, and are set out as an indication to some belated plane to guide it home.

These lights of the Front! To what untiring watchfulness they bear witness! The Front never sleeps.

And yet one more light before we reach our destination. We are nearing the town, and presently a red light appears in the centre of the road. It is the barrier. For at night every entrance to the town is barred. None may go out and none come in unchallenged.

So the car slows down to pass the sentry. "Who are you?" comes the call from the darkness. We give our unit in reply.

"Right, sir, pass," comes the answer; the barrier is lifted, and we jolt along on the last stage of our journey over the rough *pavé* through the black darkness of the town.

THE OFFENSIVE BEGINS

CHAPTER IX

THE OFFENSIVE BEGINS

It was the afternoon of Good Friday, and the day had brought us a short interval of quiet and rest. In the beautiful little chapel attached to a Church Army hut a few miles behind the line, a small group in khaki were gathered together for the Three Hours' Service. The big British guns in their secret emplacements close by were silent for the moment. The German shells had ceased to scream overhead, and, in that little quiet corner at least, it seemed as though the sacredness of the day were being respected.

It was wonderful to note the calm confidence of our men in those tremendous days out in France; but for all that, they were necessarily days of anxiety. And in this anxiety those who were directing the work of the Church Army in the front areas had their full share. I cannot speak at first hand of the terrible experiences in the district swept by the German advance in the valley of the Somme, where hut after hut which had been erected in this ruined country to serve our men was overwhelmed by the onrush of the enemy. The superintendents in some cases barely escaped with their lives. Some of them were wounded. The huts were lost. An appeal has gone out to the Church at home to make good these losses, and to supply our men once more with happy, healthy places of recreation and centres of spiritual work, and this appeal must not be made in vain.

The big southern " push " which engulfed Albert, Bapaume, and Péronne, lay outside my district, and I do not propose now to tell its story. I can, however, tell our people at home something of what the Church, through this handmaid of hers, the Church Army, was doing in the Army area which flanks the invaded district. Head-quarters, from which the Commissioner of the Church Army worked in his supervision of the huts, were situated at that time in a country town no great distance from the trenches. Here were concentrated a large depot of stores—cigarettes, tobacco, biscuits, soaps, tea, matches, milk, and all sorts of commodities of the kind that a soldier loves. These were sent out in lorries, limbers, or G.S. wagons to the various huts to supply the canteens. In this centre the Commissioner lived.

Usually one is able to count on being reasonably comfortable in a town behind the lines, provided that one is not so foolish as to billet near the railway station or close to a centre of traffic, such as the junction of important roads. Railway stations invariably get shelled, and their neighbourhood is notoriously unhealthy. Street corners are interesting as places where we can see life, but the more interesting they are from this point of view, the more desirable it becomes to avoid them. The most forlorn and desolate place in the town in which I lived was a street corner at which was situated the wreckage of an *estaminet* bearing the sign of "Au Bon Coin." No house anywhere near had a pane of glass remaining intact, and hardly one was inhabited. One felt that irony could hardly go farther!

As a rule, we may sleep in our billets in peace. "Let me know at once if Fritz drops a shell into the town," said the Colonel of the neighbouring Heavies to our new Town Major, "and he will get his own back straight away, with something more. Of course he can knock the railway station as much as he likes; that is fair game; but if he strafes the civies, just ring me up."

Now, the Town Major's clerk was a very excitable youth, and "got the wind up" on the slightest provocation. The merest rumour of a raid was sufficient to send him scuttling to his dug-out, and nothing would induce him to come out till everything was quiet.

One day a gunnery school was making certain tests in the *Champs des Manœuvres* not far from the Town Major's office. These involved the explosion of a bomb, which went off with a tremendous concussion.

Sergeant Tremolow rushed out of his office and seized the telephone. "X Y Z Siege Battery — Hullo, are you the Heavies ? — Sergeant Tremolow speaking—Town Major's Office—Is the C.O. there ?—Right, I'll hang on—Oh, is that you, sir ?—The Boche has just sent a 12-inch shell over—It exploded just behind the *Place*—No, I don't know yet how many women and children have been killed—Very well, sir, —Thank you, sir—I knew you would wish to be told."

Half an hour later the Town Major came in, and the sergeant, still as white as a sheet, told him what he had done.

" But by this time," he added, " the Boche

will be sorry. The Colonel was going to put two 12-inches into M—— by way of reprisal."

The Town Major, however, heard his sergeant's story with consternation :

" Shells ? " he said, " there have been no shells in the town to-day. It is the Boche who will do the reprisals. We had better look out. We shall certainly get it here before long."

And sure enough, before the afternoon was over, eight 12-inch high explosives had fallen into our unfortunate town.

The Town Major's sergeant lost his stripes !

That incident, however, was merely an interlude in a time of quiet. It served the useful purpose of reminding us that there was a war on, and that much more exciting times could not be long delayed. Fritz, in fact, was preparing a concert on a grand scale, and the overture, we knew, would soon begin.

It was indeed a strange Passion-tide this year, for the whole front was palpitating with activity for days before the push began. The

Boche wished, so far as possible, to disguise his intentions; and in order to create uncertainty as to where his real effort would be made, he set to work to plaster the whole of the back area with shells indiscriminately up and down the line. The town of A——, which afforded a precarious shelter to the Church Army, came in for special attention, owing to its close proximity to the line. The Paschal moon gave a fine opportunity to the bombing planes, and the opportunity was not missed. Day and night the town was shelled with heavy stuff, and many were the inoffensive houses of civilians that were destroyed by this wanton " strafe."

It was a curious sensation to sit in a cellar at night listening to the shells. First came the crash of the shell hitting its victim ; then the long moaning scream of its passage through the air. For the shell travels much faster than the sound, and so the noise of its passage is left behind. Then, as the moaning dies down, comes the explosion, which takes place about five seconds after concussion. This delay is secured by means of a time-fuse, which is fired by the concussion. Its purpose is to give the shell time to penetrate into the interior of the building before it explodes. Its destructive effect is thus immensely increased.

Such was our life through Passion-tide till Maundy Thursday. And then came a lull. The big offensive was launched, and so the side shows ceased. We were able to come up from our cellars and dug-outs and breathe freely.

But what was happening to the Church Army huts down south within reach of the great battle? It was necessary to go and see. So let me take you to a hut on the edge of the battlefield, as I saw it on Maundy Thursday. It stands in the centre of an encampment in a ruined district, the last word in desolation. It is there to provide recreation for the men, in a neighbourhood where no other means of recreation is to be found. It gives them a little spot of beauty and brightness where everything around is ugly and horrible. The twisted iron framework of a broken sugar refinery faces it across the road. Rows of Nissen huts, camouflaged out of all recognition, make the landscape more hideous still. Old trenches and barbed-wire entanglements scar the ground. And in these surroundings the hut gives our lads a reminder of home. Here they write their letters. Here in moments of utter weariness they come to rest. Here in the evenings of Holy Week they have seen on the lantern screen the pictures of the Saviour's Passion. Here on Sundays evenings at the voluntary service the hut is so packed with men from end to end that many have to be refused admission.

The hut stands on rising ground, commanding a wonderful view of a long low ridge, whose name is among the glories of the British arms in this awful war. On Maundy Thursday I stood on the bank beside the hut with the superintendent, and we watched the terrific battle. All along the line of the ridge the

German shells were bursting, throwing up huge clouds of black smoke and dirt. They were falling heavily on the ruins of a village just in front of us, and were searching the slopes of the hill to find our hidden gun emplacements. The double slope, facing us and falling away at our feet, was ablaze with the fire of the British guns. Flash followed flash incessantly, now here, now there. It was a tremendous artillery duel. Not a human being was to be seen except on the road, where the crowded ranks of transport passed to and fro.

"What will you do?" I asked my superintendent.

"Oh, I shall hang on as long as I can, and then I shall set fire to the hut and go."

"Well, don't lose your head and burn the place down unnecessarily," I said with a smile.

"No, I won't do that," was his quiet reply.

And I felt sure that he could be trusted to hang on, so long as it was wise to do so. The

Church Army will stay on that battle front so long as it is able to do its work!

I left my friend watching the shells and made my way to a village, where I was to meet the D.A.C.G. of the corps at his billet at 1 p.m. When I got to the house I found an enormous shell-hole in the roadway immediately opposite to it, and a dozen soldiers working to fill it up and repair the road. The house was a ruin! I climbed the broken staircase and found the D.A.C.G.'s room a mass of débris. I went into the beautiful little chapel on the ground floor; its fittings were utterly ruined. I learnt that the shell had fallen an hour before. I was glad that my appointment had not been for 12 o'clock!

Heavy shells were still falling in the village, for the enemy evidently imagined that it sheltered some place of military importance. The villagers were rushing away, taking with them such of their belongings as they were able to carry. One poor woman was carrying a sick child, while another clung to her skirts. I picked them up in my car and carried them to a place of safety.

Just outside this village the Church Army has a hut. I went to see how it fared. I found that shells had been dropping close by, and the superintendent had evacuated it, leaving a notice on the door, " Closed; gone to ——," mentioning a country town which we will call X. I went on to X in the car, and sat down in the Church Army hut there to wait for his arrival. Presently he came in, wearing his tin hat and covered in dust from head to foot. Walking when necessary, and getting a lift when he could, he had managed to get through. I told him to stay at X, and try and keep in touch with his hut, and be guided by events. The next day a telephone message came through from him : "Hut at —— will be reopened to-morrow."

Such is the spirit of the Church Army in France ! It is not surprising that the Church Army should be winning in an ever-increasing degree the affection and respect of men at the

Front.   The Church at home can do no better work in these critical days than enable the work of these huts to go forward and grow.   It makes the men say, "The old Church at home has not forgotten us. See what she is doing for us here!"

IN THE STORM OF SHELLS

CHAPTER X

IN the outskirts of A—— is a triangular open space which we will disguise under the name of the *Place du Commerce*. It is the old market-place of A——. In the middle of its central façade a large building had been recently secured to house the rapidly growing Church Army stores. Only part of the building was available for the purpose, for it had been struck by a shell in an earlier bombardment and the upper story was in ruins. However, by the law of averages, it seemed unlikely that it would be struck again, and it was very conveniently placed. So I decided to rent what remained of it for the modest sum of one franc per day.

The two other sides of this triangular space

contained respectively my office and garage. I
mention this now as the fact is interesting in the
light of subsequent events.

Monday, April 8th, was the calm before the
storm. In the *Place du Commerce* the stalls for
the weekly market were being set up ready for
the display of goods for sale.

In peace time and in the earlier days of the
war, after the fear caused by the first bombardment of A—— had died down, this market
was a wonderful sight. The big *Place* was
completely covered by the stalls and booths.
From the whole countryside the farmers were
accustomed to bring in their country produce
for sale. Shopkeepers from other little towns near
by would bring in a cart-load of stores from their
stock, with a view to adding to their local gains
by tapping the financial resources of the people of
A——. It was a lively scene, and the surround-
ing *estaminets* were wont to do a thriving trade.

But, alas! those spacious days had gone by
and the Monday market had lost its prosperity,

for only adventurous souls would bring their goods to a centre where at any time they might be dispersed by a shell.

So on Monday, April 8th, though the stalls were there, the market retained but a shadow of its former beauty. The few stalls that were erected were gathered side by side in one corner of the big *Place*, as though crouching together for mutual protection.

The superintendents of the neighbouring Church Army huts came in as usual that morning to see the Commissioner, bringing with them their weekly reports and their bags of money to pay into the central account. They ordered their weekly supplies from the Church Army stores, to be delivered at their huts the next day by motor-lorry, and then returned to their huts in peace and quiet.

By the kindness of the military authorities a capital system of distribution of goods to the canteens in the various huts has been arranged. Each Corps in this Army is ready to send a lorry to the Church Army stores at A——— whenever it may be required, to take out goods to the huts in the Corps area. In this way our huts are kept well supplied.

On Monday afternoons, after the superintendents have gone, it is the work of the storekeeper to make up the consignments of goods that have been ordered, so that they may be ready for the Corps' lorries when they come next day. But this time, alas! the goods from our stores were not destined to reach the huts for which they were intended. Before they could be delivered, the storm had burst.

The story of two days crowded with excitement and tragedy and tales of heroism is worth telling. The morning of April 9th was ushered in by a terrific bombardment. A thick fog lay over the fen stretches, where the water is so close to the surface that no real trench can be dug, and little protection is afforded by the shallow breastworks which alone are possible. The Boche was preparing for an attack under cover

of the mist.   To prevent the arrival of reinforcements he was throwing shells into A——, and
trying to block the main arteries of traffic.

It was the anniversary of the capture by the
Canadians of the Vimy Ridge, and therefore a
happy day, as I thought, to visit the Canadian
area and get news of the welfare of the huts in
that district.   The part of the line to be visited
was one which for certain reasons possessed a
high strategic importance, and was of corres-
ponding danger to the huts involved.   So I
started off through the streets of the town.
Hardly a soul was to be seen, for more Boche
shells were expected over at any moment.   It
was such a ride as Lady Godiva's through the
streets of Coventry, "Peeping Tom's" part
being represented by furtive glances from cellars
and dug-outs.

Presently it became clear that the direct way
was barred.   The ruins of a house lay right
across the road.   There was nothing for it but
to turn back and try another exit from the town.

This time we were more successful, and were soon speeding through the open country towards the edge of the battlefield.

Needless to say we found the Canadians with their " tails well up " on this anniversary, which among many splendid achievements marks the day of special Canadian glory. The Boche has learnt to have a very healthy respect for the Canadians, and he has come to believe that he has little chance against a fort which the Canadians hold ! It would indeed be a tonic for faint hearts, if there are any such among us, to make the tour I made on April 9th through the Canadian area, to talk to the lads in our huts and to the A.D.C.S. (Assistant Director of Chaplains' Service) at Canadian Head-quarters, and to see the splendid spirit that animated them all.

It was middle afternoon when I got back to my shell-swept town. A broad avenue leads to the *Place du Commerce*. The *Place*, as we saw it at the end of the Boulevard, was thick with a cloud of yellow dust. What did this mean ?

We were not left in doubt when we turned the corner and entered the big square. The Church Army stores were in ruins. A shell of very large calibre had fallen on the building a few minutes before.

We made our way inside. What a scene of wreckage! The central passage, which is a carriage-way to the courtyard and coachhouse at the rear, was thick with the ruins of the ceiling. A piano, waiting to go out to a new hut, was buried deep. The doors of the rooms on either side had been blown off their hinges by the concussion. The shell had struck the wall on the side of the courtyard and ripped it open in its passage through, to bury itself in the packing-cases within.

Imagine those sinister seconds during which, after concussion, the fuse was burning! Then the roar of explosion! From back to front the big house was burst through; in the courtyard the coachhouse, with its store, lay in ruins. And, crowning tragedy, in the coachhouse the

Church Army storekeeper lay dead, his body stretched across a packing-case over the threshold whither he had rushed in those awful moments after the falling of the shell and before it burst!

Ah! the Church Army has some faithful servants. And here was one who had died at the post of duty. I know well that his heart was in his work, and I am mourning a real friend through his death. His body was laid to rest in the cemetery beyond the canal outside the town.

In this beautiful cemetery, a veritable God's Acre, the French General commanding the district and the Corps Commander of the British troops had stood side by side, on All Saints' Day, as the mayor pronounced his eulogy on the men of the two countries who had fallen in defence of the liberties of each.

How wonderful, how inexpressibly touching, these war cemeteries are, with their long rows of wooden crosses! On one side of the central path the tricolour rosettes tell of the *poilus* who lie beneath the soil; on the other are the British graves, where each name is carefully recorded on the cross standing at the head. The union of the two in that last long resting-place is the symbol of their unity in the struggle for the same great ideal which is drawing together all the free peoples of the world.

In that cemetery on the banks of the canal the body of the little Church Army storekeeper has been laid to rest.

All through the night of April 9th a rain of shells was falling in almost unbroken continuity on the doomed town. The cellar in which we took refuge reverberated with the constant crashes; first the crunching sound as the shell pierced its victim, and then the explosion and the crumbling of masonry as the house fell in ruins. As I listened through the long hours of the night, it seemed as though little could be left of the town in the morning. I wondered whether I should see the great square tower of

the parish church still dominating the town, or
the quaint old belfry in the Grande Place when
the dawn returned. The next day they still
stood proudly above the ruins of the streets.
But who shall say how much longer they can
escape this ruthless assault?

The Boche was straining every nerve to break
through the line we so tenaciously held. And
through all the hours of the day there were two
steady streams on the road. On the one hand
the wounded were coming down, some of them
walking, others in ambulances to the casualty
clearing stations; and there was convoy after
convoy of prisoners brought down from the line.
And in the other direction reinforcements were
crowding up to the trenches.

It is a very wonderful sight to see a regiment
marching up to take its place in the line of battle.
At one point the traffic on the road was held up
to allow a very splendid Highland regiment to
pass. Each man knew what the battle meant;
each man knew it would be hell. Yet how

CHURCH ARMY STORES AFTER THE BOMBARDMENT OF ————————

proudly and fearlessly they held themselves as they swung along with smiling faces, and to the refrain of a Highland song!

It is just as real an heroism, though without the exultation of battle, which our hut-workers were showing at this time. The news came through to me that day of a hut in the danger area. A shell had fallen a few yards away from the hut : one of those high-explosive shells which in addition to the explosive contain also a chamber of poison gas—surely one of the enemy's last devices in devilish ingenuity. The hut-workers had come away, having been evacuated by order of their Town Major. One of them was in hospital from the gas fumes; the other declared that he was ready to go back and re-open the hut for the boys as soon as the situation cleared.

The Church Army had already at that early period of the offensive lost fifty-five huts in the southern push. Here, then, was another nearly added to the tale!

A REFUGEE

CHAPTER XI

A REFUGEE

WEDNESDAY, April 10th, found the battle for A—— raging fast and furious. All through the night the shells had been falling into the town, and the place had become quite uninhabitable. It was time to go!

It only remained for me to pick up so much of my office files and furniture as my car would carry and go out into the wilderness to seek a fresh home.

But whither? It was not easy to find fresh quarters, for all the little towns and the villages in the neighbourhood were either crowded out with refugees from the shelled area or packed with troops. It was necessary to seek a friend

at court and ask for a new roof to shelter myself
and my staff.

So I took the car out to the quiet country
village where the Head-quarters of the Corps
were installed.

I walked through the French window into the
room in which the "Q" staff of the Corps were
at work.

The room was bare of all but the immediate
necessities for work. Everything not required at
the moment was packed up and put away, for
at critical times such as this, even a Corps
Head-quarters must be ready to flit at a moment's
notice. If the push on our portion of the Front
were successful, the villages behind the line
would quickly become too unhealthy to admit
of the staff continuing their work. A park of
lorries had to be held in readiness in case Corps
Head-quarters might be required to move.

At one end of the room was a vast large-scale
map of the Corps area. A multitude of little
flags of varied colours and designs were pinned

into it, marking the position of every detail in the complicated scheme that constituted the fighting machine of the Corps.

I had just come from the battle front, where the Boche was straining every nerve. I was now to see something of the working of a battle behind the scenes.

The staff officer to whom I addressed myself looked up from his table.

"Hullo, Commissioner," he said, "what can I do for you? Can't give you much time. We have got this battle on, and we are all sitting at the end of telephones, pushing it through."

The telephone bell rang, and my friend took up the receiver.

"Yes, 'Q' office speaking. You want ten thousand 18-lb. shrapnel? Right you are. Send over to Blazes Dump for them; I will ring them up and authorise delivery."

Another ring.

"Hullo, is that 888 Machine-gun Company?

I have already ordered five thousand belts to be sent up to you. They should be on their way by now."

Next a dispatch rider hurries in, clad in leather jacket and helmet and covered with dust from head to foot. He is from Brigade Head-quarters, at a point on the line where a critical situation seemed likely to develop. His dispatch called for immediate attention and reply.

At last a moment was found to deal with my case, and I carried away from Corps Head-quarters a chit addressed to the Town Major of the village of L——, which I had selected as best adapted to my needs.

I reached L——, with so much of my belongings as I had been able to bring away. It was late in the afternoon, and I at once called on the Town Major. A chit from Corps is an " Open Sesamé " everywhere in the Corps area, and I soon found myself in possession of a spacious garret, officially described as a billet for " Two officers and two men."

Its only means of light and ventilation was a tiny skylight in the roof; but refugees, like beggars, cannot be choosers, and I felt myself fortunate to have been able to get under a roof at all!

I cannot help recording the extraordinary kindness with which I was received. The " C. of E." padre invited me to become a member of his mess, which already sheltered the Roman Catholic and Wesleyan chaplains, both of whom were lamenting the loss of their Soldiers' Clubs in the stricken town of A——.

The Wesleyan padre was specially in trouble, because in the hurry of evacuation his orderlies had left behind the greater part of their equipment in the Club and a number of possessions which he specially valued, including his Communion vessels.

It was my intention the next morning to make a dash into A—— in the car for further salvage from my own office and stores. So I offered to take the padre's corporal with me and bring away at the same time as much as possible from the Wesleyan Club.

It was difficult to thread one's way along the roads, which were thronged with troops and transport going up to the line and with refugees coming away from villages near the front.

I can imagine few sights more pathetic than this stream of refugees. One who had been out in France since the beginning of the war said he had seen nothing like it since the Retreat from Mons. There were carts loaded up with swaying furniture; kitchen utensils, parlour ornaments, live poultry, and garden tools, all tied on in apparently inextricable confusion. There were heavy carts drawn by horses and smaller vehicles to which donkeys were harnessed; some were dragged by dogs, others by old men and women. Others, again, were pulled even by little children. Cattle were being driven along the roads. Sometimes an old grandmother would be seen riding on the foot-board of a cart piled high with the household gods; more often the refugees had to walk or limp by the side.

And how greatly they added to the difficulty of getting along the road! The Frenchman has an inveterate habit of driving in the centre of the road, even if he is not actually on the wrong side. Often our transport would be delayed by a block created by these poor creatures, distraught by the loss of their home and dazed by their journey out into the unknown.

We turned aside to visit a hut that seemed likely to come into the line of the German advance. It was in the low water-logged ground to the north. In nine years out of ten an advance over this country would have been a practical impossibility at this early season of the year. It is a tract over which it is impossible to cut deep trenches, as the water level is reached almost at once. The utmost that can be done is to scratch the soil and throw up a shallow breastwork. After rain such a district as this becomes quite impossible for the traction of guns.

But this year the weather was fine and the ground was dry. It was an extraordinary piece of good fortune for the German offensive!

In this swampy district very large numbers of our troops had been billeted, and a Church Army hut had been erected in their midst. It was necessary to raise up the hut on piles, and it stood out above the marshy ground like a lake-dwelling of prehistoric times.

What a story the superintendent had to tell us! Men who had held the line in the southern push had been sent back to his billet to rest. This was before the outbreak of the northern battle had made this area as unhealthy as it subsequently became.

The men had crowded into the hut, utterly tired out, and told of their experience down south.

" We did nothing but kill Germans," they said, " for hour after hour. We went on killing them in heaps, till we were sick of it. They came on in massed formation, wave after wave, and we just mowed them down with our machine guns and rifles; you couldn't help killing them. They fell like flies. Talk of slaughter! Their later waves had to climb over stacks of corpses to get to us. And it seemed like butchery; we were sick and tired of it before it was done."

These were men who had held the southern line at a crucial point where the Germans had been instructed at all costs to break through. The Boche had indeed paid the price, but the goods had not been delivered!

On the day of our visit to this hut conditions had changed. Once again it was crowded to the doors, this time by men who had been brought back from the immediate front for a short rest. Many of them were famished, for it is not always easy to get rations through punctually when a battle is on.

It was already nearly midday, but the superintendent of the hut had had no breakfast that morning; he had been at work continuously, attending to the wants of the men. Many of them had no money ; they received free gifts of biscuits and tea. Often when they had drunk their tea they would throw themselves down on the floor of the hut, and in a moment would be sound asleep.

The superintendent had some news which was ominous for the hut.

" A battery of heavy guns has been set up a couple of hundred yards away. That means that the hut and village will soon be laid flat."

Experience has shown us only too clearly that when guns are put down in the neighbourhood of a hut, the hut's days are numbered, for very soon the guns draw the enemy's fire.

One of the principal objects of the air service is to detect the gun positions of the enemy. Every gun emplacement is of course carefully camouflaged to make it as difficult as possible to detect. But a slight shadow on the photograph taken from the air may reveal the gun, or it may be spotted by means of its flash.

The gun may also be located by noting the

exact moment at which the sound of the firing reaches two points of observation. When the difference in the time has been calculated the gun is known to be situated in a certain geometric curve.

By taking two other points of observation a second curve can be traced on the map, upon which the gun must lie.

The emplacement of the gun is then known to be at the point at which these two curves intersect.

Thus, a gun position, perhaps ten miles away, can be almost exactly located mathematically without any direct observation from the air. Then, when the position is known, the music begins! And presently, if the gun is not knocked out, it has to be taken away.

So, when I heard that British batteries had been set up near this hut of ours at H——, I knew that the hut would soon be knocked out. Indeed, I learnt shortly afterwards that the C.O. had come the next day to the superintendent, and had told him that he must close down and evacuate. Probably the hut has become match-wood long ere this !

A feature of this offensive has been the free use of gas. A certain battalion noticed that they were receiving large rations of pork. This was at first regarded as a welcome change from " bully," and the men wondered to what this unwonted burst of generosity on the part of the supply department was due. Presently it became known that all the pigs in a neighbouring village had been gassed the week before. Since then the 10th King's Own Scorchers have been apt to regard fresh pork as suspect !

A CITY OF DEATH

CHAPTER XII

A CITY OF DEATH

THE Front is a wonderful place for rumours, which often take the form of circumstantial lies rounded off in every particular. There seems to be a sort of microbe of inventiveness which finds a favourable medium for its development in the mental atmosphere behind the lines. The most impossible stories are told with all the solemnity of gospel truth.

My journey to H—— had taken me through the village of C——, which at this time had acquired an unenviable notoriety for German attentions in the matter of shells. No place with a railway station was exactly a health resort at this time. A chaplain whom I met at F—— on the afternoon of that day had a lot to tell me about the doings of the Boche.

"Which way are you returning to L—— ?" he asked me. "You cannot, of course, go through C——. A 12-inch shell exploded in the middle of the roadway in the village two hours ago, and has made a large hole six feet deep, and there is a fatigue party of ten men working at it to get it filled up."

Having received this definite information, I naturally decided to return by another route. The next day, however, I found it necessary to go through C——. The roadway was intact from end to end of the village. It was quite certain that no shell had exploded on it the day before. Yet the padre, whose veracity was undeniable, knew the calibre of the shell that had fallen, the exact time of the occurrence, the depth of the hole that had been made, and the number of men who were engaged in filling it in! It was as fine an example as one could wish to find of a really full-blown circumstantial lie!

CHURCH ARMY OFFICE AFTER THE BOMBARDMENT OF ――――――

The Boche, however, was trying hard to rectify this little mistake when I was going through C—— the next day. A shell actually fell in the village just in front of my car. It was at an angle in the roadway, and the house at the corner was struck just as I was passing. Fortunately the front of the house resisted the explosion and no fragments reached the road. But my driver crowded on full speed till we were clear of this very unhealthy locality!

After our visit to the hut at H—— we continued our journey to A——. Shells were falling intermittently into the town as we rushed at full speed through the *faubourg* to the *Place du Commerce*. We left the car under the lee of the eastern side of the square, where it would be in comparative safety, and then began to take stock of the position.

Facing us across the *Place* was the Church Army garage. It was a ruin, absolute and complete. A big shell had fallen on it during the previous night, and it lay flat on the ground!

11

By a happy chance it was empty. My spare
car had been there for a whole month, waiting
for certain spare parts to arrive from England.
These parts just then were most difficult to pro-
cure; but they had arrived two days before,
and the car had been sent at once into the
Army repair shop to be refitted. It was
indeed a piece of luck.

I hurried round the corner, hoping to pick
up some private belongings from my billet. The
two houses next but one to mine were in ruins,
and my own house was locked and deserted.
All was silent as the grave in that street of
death.

I next made my way to my office to collect
some important papers, and was met by my
friend the corporal who had been sent in with
me to save what he could from the Wesleyan
Club.

He arrived breathless, laden with equipment.
He had hoped to find some soldier on police
duty in the town to help him to carry his pro-

perty. But there was no one to be found, and he reported that a shell had fallen and exploded close at hand just as he was coming away.

It was impossible to take the car any nearer, as the streets were blocked with débris, so I ran with him to the Club to rescue another load. We found the Communion vessels, which I thrust into my pocket, and then made a selection of what seemed most valuable. We hurried back to the car, carrying what we could. It was getting too hot to stay any longer, so we started the car and dashed back into the open country.

There remained the problem of my own stores. About £2,000 worth of cigarettes, biscuits, tea, and other goods were lying there in the ruins. The door, displaced by the explosion, had refused to lock, but I had managed to secure it by means of a chain and padlock to prevent looting.

How were all these valuable stores to be rescued ? I visited another hut to consult the superintendent as to ways and means. He said that if the Corps would lend him a lorry he would watch his opportunity when the shelling died down and would make a dash into A—— to bring away as much as he could. The Corps, ever ready to help, agreed to do this.

The next day I paid a further visit to this hut, and found, in the roadway outside, a Corps lorry packed to its utmost capacity with goods salvaged from the stores.

The superintendent had a thrilling story to tell. The Boche was shelling the town with shrapnel; but my friend had taken a fatigue party with him, so that the lorry might be loaded up in the shortest possible time, and they had returned triumphant.

Other journeys were subsequently undertaken, and soon these sorely needed stores were distributed through the Church Army huts. This was at a time when it was absolutely impossible to obtain any fresh stores from England. The men, returning famished from the trenches, were clamouring for biscuits and tea. It was a tremendous boon to them that we were able to supply them so abundantly at this difficult time. In this task of rescue the Canadian Corps gave us most generous and ready help, which I wish to take this opportunity of acknowledging.

I paid one more visit to A——, this time taking with me the official photographer. I found that by this time my office had gone the way of the stores and garage. A shell, evidently a very heavy one, had struck the building. It was a complete ruin. The whole of the front had collapsed except the front door and about two feet of brickwork at its side. On this fragment of wall the Church Army sign still remained intact!

All the furniture of the upper floor, the beds and wardrobes, lay in a confused heap on my front office. Nothing remained intact except the portraits of Sir John French and Prebendary Carlile, which were still hanging in their places on the wall!

I found it impossible to open the front door, but I was able to look through into the passage.

It was one of those French doors whose panels are fitted with a large iron grating. Through the grating I could take stock of the débris within. A hole, five feet wide, pierced the floor of the hall. It was evident that a second shell had struck the building and had penetrated the brick vaulting of the cellar and exploded within it. The force of the explosion had lifted the floor, to form a ridge down the centre of the hall. It was this ridge which prevented my opening the door.

It was in this cellar that I had often sat to do my office work in the evening when a raid was on. It would only have been a death-trap after all!

It was a curious coincidence that all three buildings associated with my work were thus laid in ruins. It seemed as though the Boche had a special spite against the Church Army! And indeed from his point of view he might be forgiven if this were so. For it is the work of voluntary associations, of which the Church

Army is one, which has done so much to keep up the spirits of the men and so to increase their value as a fighting force.

The Church Army alone lost over a hundred huts in the spring offensive. We have never hesitated to place our huts as near to the line as prudence, or the military authorities, would allow; for it is in the shelled areas that the need for them is greatest. To set up new huts and tents behind the new British line at least £100,000 will be required. The appeal for this sum will surely meet with an eager response.

The fine old church tower of A—— was still standing erect when I came away from the town on the completion of my errand; but at least three shells had struck its massive bulk. There were gaping wounds in its parapet and buttresses. The church itself was little better than a ruin.

We left the town by a beautiful avenue of stately trees. This avenue had already been marked down for destruction for our own military use, so great now is the need for timber. The trees had been blazed and numbered ready for the axe.

But a more cruel force was now laying them low. The Boche shells were playing havoc with their shapely beauty. Several of them lay broken and splintered by the side of the roadway.

Poor bleeding France! This town of death was typical of her sufferings for the moment. But none need doubt that through this trial of fire and sword a new France is rising up that shall be stronger and better than the old.

CHAPTER XIII

RECONSTRUCTION

In huts, billets, barracks, and dug-outs, up and down the Front, wherever our men gather together, there is one subject of discussion. It is the question: "What are we going back to after the war?" One thing at least is certain, that the men who have fought in France will not tolerate the old abuses in our social system and industrial life. They will refuse to return to the cramping conditions under which so many of them were living when their country called them to come out and fight her battles. There is no need to fear trouble, provided that those in authority in our country are alive to the signs of the times and are in earnest in carrying through that Reconstruction which the changed conditions of "after the war" will require.

We have to confess that under the social conditions that prevailed before the war the full human life, the life that gave real scope for the development of all the varied sides of complex human personality, was impossible for a large proportion of our population. It was not so much that wages were inadequate, though often this was the case; but the trouble rather lay in a faulty recognition of the claims of personality. We thought of the wealth-producing power of the individual rather than of the supreme value of the man or woman as a personal being. So our whole standard of values was wrong, and our social scheme, based on fundamentally false ideas, was vitiated at the start.

All our schemes of Reconstruction must be based on the assumption of the supreme value of human personality. And it is this fact, shorn of long words and technical phrases, which is

really in the minds of the men who are now so
ardently discussing the future in their billets
at the Front.

" It is not so much that we want higher wages
or shorter hours," a working man said to a
parson ; " but we want to count."

They want to be recognised as men, and not
merely as " hands " in a mill, or as parts of a
machine.   And the life in the new England
that will arise after the war will succeed or
fail just in proportion to the degree in which
it gives to all citizens of our country that
glorious freedom which allows a man to live
the wide human life in the exercise of the
faculties of body, mind, and spirit for which he
was created.

This is the freedom we are fighting to secure for
ourselves and for the small nations of the world :
the freedom for self-determination, self-develop-
ment.   This in its noblest sense is what we
mean by Democracy.   The opening of the
pathway to this goal is surely what President

Wilson had in his mind when he expressed the aim of the Allies in the war as "making the world safe for Democracy."

How, then, can this aim be secured so far as our own country is concerned ? What changes are necessary in our social system or in our industrial life ?

Not only is it true that these questions are being eagerly canvassed by our men at the Front, but it also seems as though the conditions of life at the Front are doing much to suggest directions in which the solution of some of our social problems may be sought, and possibly found. Men who have been taken out of their old surroundings, and thrown into a fresh and utterly unaccustomed life, are able to look at the old problems from a new angle. Their minds are widened. They can learn something from the social conditions of the new country in which they find themselves. Differences and controversies which bulked large in old days take on gentler outlines and appear in a truer proportion. It is easier to recognise the element of justice in the other person's point of view. All this helps to create an atmosphere conducive to the solving of difficulties. It promotes something of that goodwill which would smooth away nine-tenths of our disagreements, if it could be maintained at home.

What, then, are the changes that are necessary in our home life if the fires and furnace of war are to fulfil their cleansing office ? We may enumerate some of them, and try to see how far the conditions under which our citizen army in France is living are preparing our English manhood for a truer conception of citizenship and a wider, freer, more human life.

We want a new spirit in industrial life, a new atmosphere of co-operation and goodwill. We need to secure that the workers, whether men or women, shall be able to live under such conditions as will enable them to rejoice in their manhood and womanhood. How few, comparatively, there are who have learnt in any real degree what a wonderful and glorious thing is this human life of ours, and what an exquisite delight there is in the exercise of our best human powers and in the development of our faculties! We want this experience to be brought within the reach of all.

This implies far better housing conditions than we have yet attained in large quarters of our great cities.

Our men have been much struck by some of the Garden Cities on the Western Front. In the mining districts, for instance, they have learnt that the hardest industrial life is not incompatible with happy, healthy conditions. Towards evening we meet the miners on the roads returning from their work. They are bicycling back to their cottage homes. Their hands and faces are black from the coal-dust of the pit; but presently they will be washed and clean and ready to enjoy their evening with their family in their cottage, with its well-kept garden. There is nothing slovenly about the wife, nothing dirty in

the home.   Everything is bright and delightful.
In connection with some of the modern mines a
Garden City has been laid out near the pit-head,
and each miner has his cottage standing in his
own little plot of ground, which is always carefully tended.   The French are naturally thrifty
and industrious, and they know how to make
the best of life.

It is not merely that their external conditions
are better than those under which so many of our
people live in the back streets of our overgrown
towns, but there is a quality in the national
character which enables the French wage-earner
to take advantage of his opportunities.   His wife
knows how to keep the home clean and comfortable, and, not least, she knows how to cook ! I
cannot help thinking that men who have been
billeted in these cottage surroundings in France
will have learnt something of what cottage life
may be. My own billet for over six months was
in a small cottage in a street largely occupied
by miners.   It was my custom when my work

was over for the day to sit with my hosts in their little kitchen and to discuss with them, over coffee and tobacco, the social and political problems of France and her hope of a new life after the war. They were deeply religious people, and were full of indignation at the repressive policy adopted by the Government of their country in recent years. It seems quite clear that this policy does not represent the real mind of France, and that the Church will occupy a much stronger position when the war is over. When the priests come back from the trenches, where they have fought so loyally and have won unstinted admiration, they will possess a power and influence in their country, new not merely in degree, but in kind.

It will be an influence quite different from that which the Roman priests in Ireland, for instance, exert over an uneducated population. It will be an influence born of contact with real life, and it will be felt beyond the limit of those who are usually disposed to acknowledge the authority of the Church. There is every reason to hope that the claims of religion will make themselves felt in that Reconstruction which France also must undertake when the war is over. We must see to it that the same shall be true of our own country as well.

Life in France should have taught our men much as to the possibilities of rural life. Everywhere they have seen evidences of the happy working of the system of peasant proprietorship. Let us walk along the street of a French village in which several hundreds of our men are billeted. We shall pass farm after farm on either side, as we go up the street.

Through a large gateway we enter the farmyard. On one side are the barns and cowsheds ; on the other, built usually on a raised terrace, is the long low farmhouse itself. The door brings us straight into the kitchen, with its large fireplace adapted to the special requirements of a farmer's cooking operations. On the dresser

12

we shall probably see a row of beautiful old pewter
dishes, some a plain round, some decorated with
fillets and foliated edges.   The lady of the farm
will show them to us with pride, pointing out the
old marks on the back, probably a rose or a
crown.   She tells us that they are " souvenirs de
famille " ;   many of them date from the time of
Louis XV or Louis XVI, and have been handed
down from father to son ever since.   Under
no consideration would their owners part with
them.   Like the farm itself they are a family
heirloom.

In an English village, instead of these numerous
small farms, we find, as a rule, that the land is in
the hands of quite a few proprietors.   A large
farmhouse stands in isolated grandeur.   None
but the fortunate four or five rich folk in the
village can ever hope to be more than a labourer ;
never an owner, only a tenant.   The system is
excused by the upholders of the old order on the
ground that small farming cannot be made
to pay.

In the meantime the rural districts are being depopulated. Land before the war was being laid down as pasture, partly, no doubt, on account of the low price of corn, but also because of the increasing scarcity of labour. We are agreed that our fields must not again be allowed to fall out of cultivation. But to effect this, we shall need something more than the artificial stimulus which has been applied to agriculture to meet war necessities; we must do a great deal more to make rural life attractive under modern conditions. The countryman must not find himself excluded from those new interests which have added so much to the possibilities of life in recent years.

But also we must do much more to give him a direct interest in the soil which he tills. In this direction the French landed system has much to teach us, and our soldiers, who have seen its working at close quarters in their billets in the little farms of France, will come back to rural life in England imbued with new ideas as to what is possible in their own countryside.

Another direction in which there is need for radical reformation and reconstruction is in the provision of means of recreation and entertainment for the people. Can there be a more ghastly example of British failure to solve a social problem than the fact that for multitudes of our population the only place of social intercourse is a public-house? We recognise the evils associated with public-houses, for we hedge these places of entertainment around with all sorts of restrictions. But we allow the root-fact to remain, that the only place where men can meet their fellows for social enjoyment when work is over is a place owned and controlled by persons or companies whose only interest in it worth mentioning is the sale of intoxicating drink !

We are all agreed that this condition of things must be changed after the war. My purpose now is to point out how our soldiers' experience in France may indicate directions in which a solution may be found. It must always be borne in mind that this public-house problem is a social one; we have to consider how the social instincts of the people can be satisfied.

Now, is it not significant that among the happiest places of entertainment, recreation, and social intercourse in France are the Church Army huts ? In these huts no intoxicating drink of any kind is sold.

But wait; I must admit an exception which proves the rule. I was engaged in an exploring expedition in a new area in company with the D.A.C.G. of a Corps which had lately come in. We were prospecting the district with a view to opening out new work in whatever centres might seem most suitable. We went to visit a derelict hut, which had been abandoned in the early days of the war owing to military changes. We found the local unit in possession, and a notice chalked up outside: " N'th Brigade : Wet and Dry Canteen."

We went inside. It was the last word in desolation. No comfort or brightness; no pictures, curtains, or tables. Only some bare forms and the wreckage of a piano.

But at the end of the hut was a canteen. On one side were three huge barrels of beer; on the other a few forlorn packets of cigarettes; nothing else. A depressed corporal was handing out mugs of beer to a handful of equally depressed and silent soldiers.

Come back to this same hut at a later date. In the meantime it has been taken down and re-erected in an important centre. It is gay with bunting and pictures. It is crowded with men, smoking, eating biscuits and chocolate, or drinking tea. The tables are occupied by little groups, talking, playing games, writing letters, or reading magazines. Neither is there any sale of intoxicating drink, nor apparently is the want of it felt. The building has been restored to its use as a Church Army hut.

Here emphatically is an institution which has solved the social problem at the Front. Cannot this suggest lines on which the same problem might be tackled at home ? It has been proved quite conclusively that social enjoyment does not depend on beer.

It would be beyond the scope of this book to attempt anything like a complete examination of all the directions in which Reconstruction will be needed after the war. I have only sought to indicate certain ways in which light seems to have been thrown upon these problems by an experience at the Front. This, however, should be added : that if Reconstruction is to be effective, there must be developed among us a higher ideal of citizenship and a deeper sense of the responsibilities it entails. Not only must we fight " to make the world safe for Democracy," but, as Bishop Brent reminded a great gathering of chaplains at the Front, we must struggle " to make Democracy safe for the world."

The *débâcle* in Russia has shown us how disastrous is an untaught Democracy, which knows neither discipline nor restraint. We have learnt much through the discipline of suffering, through the blood and tears of war. The bitter lesson must not have been given in vain.

But we shall never succeed in our social ideals unless through the power of religion. Fundamentally our aim must be the coming of the Kingdom of God; and the preaching of this Kingdom is the mission of the Church.

How, then, is the Church, in the years that are coming, to get such a grip upon the national life as to make her voice heard and her call obeyed ? There must be a new vitality in her work and worship; she must show that she really cares for the welfare of the people; she must interpret her ancient principles and doctrines in the light of truths which modern knowledge has unfolded.

While maintaining her continuity with the past, she must get rid of the spirit of antiquarianism, which is fatal to progress; she must put aside the dead controversies and trivial bickerings, which bulk far too largely in the thoughts of her professed adherents; she must make her services real to modern ears; she must attain a truer sense of proportion, putting first things first, and allowing things of secondary importance to fall back into their proper place; she must develop a new sense of fellowship within her own borders; she must approach in a new spirit the problem of " our unhappy divisions."

On this last point our life in France has taught us much. The spirit of fellowship and comradeship has been wonderfully developed among all ranks at the Front. An extraordinary bond of union exists between those who have shared together the life of the trenches, who together have been " over the top," and who when their job in the line is finished have come back together for recreation and rest.

In spite of the military discipline which sets a dividing line between officers and men, there has been a quite remarkable breaking down of class distinctions; a new Democracy has grown up in the Service. For officers are now drawn from all classes; generally speaking, every one now seeking a commission must first have served in the ranks. All this tends to give a broader outlook to the Officers' Mess. It strengthens the bond of sympathy; for the officers know their men.

Thus, there has grown up at the Front a deepened sense of comradeship, which will demand continued expression in civil life after the war. How shall this expression be found? We shall look for it in trades unions and clubs; but surely not only there. Why should we not also find it in the Church? Indeed, will not the influence of the Church depend very largely on her power to make her fellowship real? A new spirit of Democracy must be brought into her councils, giving to all her members the opportunity of self-expression, the exercise of a real citizenship, the bearing of a true responsibility ; each congregation must exhibit the life of a large and happy family united in a true comradeship, constantly seeking fresh members and bringing them within the circle of its own family life.

But what of our relation to other Christian bodies ? Here, again, we may learn something from our experience at the Front. We cannot go back again to our old position of misunderstanding and aloofness. We must struggle for a new unity : at least of spirit. How happy have been the relations between the different denominations in France ! Always there has been goodwill. There has been the recognition that to men of different temperaments and different training, different forms of worship and different types of service will appeal. Sometimes there has been actual co-operation between chaplains of different denominations in those voluntary evening services in the Recreation huts, which have won so splendid a response from the men. Thus, one chaplain will take the prayers and read the lessons, the other preaching the sermon. Sometimes chaplains of two denominations, whose work lies in the same centre, have preferred to take the whole service in turns on alternate Sundays, saying that they thus feel freer in the exercise of their ministry. But always there is the spirit of goodwill. Any bickering or disagreement would be regarded paltry beyond words in the presence of the tremendous realities of life and death that occupy our minds at the Front.

In these services in France we possess a liberty of experiment which could only be made at home by defying ecclesiastical authority. There is thus a special value in our services at the Front. They should be fruitful in suggestion as to how best our Church life in the home country may be amended to bring it into harmony with modern needs. The religious experience of our soldiers in France may help us to solve the problem of how the Church may be enabled to take her true place in the new England that shall be built up after the war.

ND - #0158 - 270225 - C0 - 198/129/12 - PB - 9781910500224 - Matt Lamination